The Limits of Identity

BORDER HISPANISMS
JON BEASLEY-MURRAY, ALBERTO MOREIRAS,
AND GARETH WILLIAMS, SERIES EDITORS

The Limits of Identity

POLITICS AND POETICS
IN LATIN AMERICA

Charles Hatfield

University of Texas Press　　Austin

Requests for permission to reproduce material from this work should be
sent to:
    Permissions
    University of Texas Press
    P.O. Box 7819
    Austin, TX 78713-7819
    http://utpress.utexas.edu/index.php/rp-form

♾ The paper used in this book meets the minimum requirements of
ANSI/NISO Z39.48-1992 (R1997) (Permanence of Paper).

LIBRARY OF CONGRESS CATALOGING-IN-PUBLICATION DATA
Hatfield, Charles Dean, 1977– author.
    The limits of identity : politics and poetics in Latin America /
Charles Hatfield. — First edition.
        pages   cm — (Border Hispanisms)
    Includes bibliographical references and index.
    ISBN 978-1-4773-0543-0 (cloth : alk. paper) — ISBN 978-1-4773-0729-8
(pbk. : alk. paper) — ISBN 978-1-4773-0544-7 (library e-book) —
ISBN 978-1-4773-0545-4 (nonlibrary e-book)
    1. Latin America—Civilization.   2. Group identity—Latin America.
I. Title.
    F1414.3.H38   2015
    980—dc23   2015010196

doi:10.7560/305430

Contents

Acknowledgments

I WOULD NEVER HAVE STARTED OR FINISHED THIS book had it not been for the advice and support I received from colleagues, friends, and family—more people than I can possibly thank here.

The first course I took with Keith Ellis while I was an undergraduate set me on the path I am on today, and in a very real way, this book started with him. Virtually every page of what follows reflects what I learned in graduate school from Eduardo González, whose intellectual courage was, and continues to be, an inspiration and example. I want to thank John Irwin, Walter Benn Michaels, and Steve Nichols for giving me the right advice at the right time. Alberto Moreiras had faith in this project from the beginning, and I have benefited in innumerable ways from our conversations over the years.

I am grateful to Bram Acosta, Sean Cotter, Eugenio Di Stefano, Shari Goldberg, Francisco Morán, Jessica Murphy, René Prieto, Emilio Sauri, Dan Wickberg, and especially Lisa Siraganian for reading and commenting on portions of the manuscript. It is a better book for their comments.

Since 2007, I have been fortunate to have an extraordinary group of friends and colleagues at the University of Texas at Dallas. Special thanks are due to Rick Brettell, Susan Briante, Farid Matuk, Peter Park, Clay Reynolds, Natalie Ring, Mark Rosen, Eric Schlereth, Rainer Schulte, Shilyh Warren, and Michael Wilson.

I am also grateful to the two anonymous readers for the University of Texas Press and to Theresa May and Kerry Webb, the two editors who saw this project through. Thanks are due to Nancy Lavender Bryan at the press for her assistance in the final steps of publication.

Nothing I do would be possible without the love, support, and example that I received from my parents, Evelyn Hatfield and the late Charles Hatfield. Finally, I want to thank Amy Freund, my ideal reader, for her love.

MATERIAL IN THIS BOOK ORIGINALLY APPEARED, IN A somewhat different form, in the following publications: "The Limits of 'Nuestra América,'" *Revista Hispánica Moderna* 63, no. 2 (2010); "The Memory Turn in Latin America," *Política Común* 6 (2014); and "From Posthegemony to Pierre Menard," *Nonsite.org* 13 (2014).

The Limits of Identity

Introduction

IN JORGE LUIS BORGES'S "CONJECTURAL POEM" (1943), Doctor Francisco Laprida reflects on his life in the moments before his violent death at the hands of "a band of gaucho militia" on September 22, 1829.[1] As bullets "whip the air" on Laprida's "last afternoon," he knows that the gauchos, whom he calls "barbarians," have won (145). Yet Laprida confesses that "a secret joy somehow swells my breast" (145). Laprida feels joy, he says, because he finds himself at last "face to face" with his "South American destiny" (145). He is dying, but he is also seeing his "true face" (145).

The fact that Laprida calls the gauchos "barbarians" evokes Domingo Faustino Sarmiento's civilization/barbarism binary pitting urban, European "civilization" against rural, autochthonous "barbarism." As Sarmiento argued in *Facundo: Civilization and Barbarism* (1845), the question facing Argentina in the middle of the nineteenth century was "to be or not to be *savages*."[2] This conception of civilization and barbarism has traditionally been criticized for its universality—for the fact, in other words, that it sees difference in terms of a universalizing disagreement about culture and politics.

The speaker in Borges's poem had devoted himself to the civilizing project in nineteenth-century Argentina, with its intrinsic universalism and attendant hierarchies. His voice had "declared the independence / of this entire untamed territory," he says, and he "longed" to "weigh / judgments, to read books, to hand down the law" (145). But as he faces his death, Laprida repudiates the beliefs that had guided his life, realizing that they had really involved the desire "to be someone else," and thus his entire life had been a "labyrinth of steps" away from his origins (145).

In Borges's poem, Laprida's desire "to be someone else" is strikingly linked with beliefs. However, his return to his presumably *real* self entails not the replacement of one set of beliefs with another but rather the replacement of beliefs with something other than belief—namely, nature, embodiment, and experience. Laprida had spent his life committed to beliefs that were thought to transcend particulars—he embraced the political ideology of independence, the law, and the world of knowledge found in books. But the path that leads him to his "South American destiny" crucially involves his body—he is overcome with blood, sweat, and pain—and the very natural world that Laprida, like Sarmiento, would have likely seen as the source of Argentina's barbarism. Thus, it is as if Borges suggests that Laprida's return to his true self is necessarily conditioned by his abandonment of beliefs in favor of his body and nature. Indeed, Laprida's discovery of his "true face" is virtually simultaneous with the ripping open of his chest and the release of his blood in the final moments of his life.

Thus, *avant la lettre*, Laprida engages what today we might call, following Walter Mignolo, "decoloniality," which dispels the "myth of universality" and proceeds from the assumption that "hierarchies are constructed [. . .] in the very process of building the idea of Western civilization and of modernity."[3] Indeed, the only adjective given to the knife that will cut Laprida's throat is "intimate" (145), despite the fact that, at least in *Facundo*, the knife is literally and figuratively synonymous with barbarism (Rosas, writes Sarmiento, "sticks the gaucho's knife into cultured Buenos Aires").[4]

Beliefs are either true or false, and the fact that a belief is ours is irrelevant to the question of whether or not it is true. In the absence of his beliefs, and the so-called "myth" of their universality, Laprida can describe things only in terms of his identity with them or experience of them. The only thing that matters about the knife is that it is his; in place of the question of whether the knife is civilized or barbaric, Laprida faces only the question of whether or not it is his—hence his sudden confrontation with his "true face" in the "night's mirror" (145).

Laprida's demise at the hands of gauchos is, in a sense, the fulfillment of what the dominant strain of Latin Americanist thought—at least since José Martí's "Nuestra América" (1891)—has desired. Laprida decolonizes himself, stripping away layers of imported practices and beliefs to allow his supposedly authentic self to come into existence. Laprida sees a circle about to "close," suggesting a fullness and completeness with his "South American destiny" that would never have been found in books or "canon law and civil [law]" (145). But inasmuch as all this is achieved with the cutting of his throat, Borges might seem to be implying that identity does not come without a high price.

That price is the subject of this book, which begins by exploring the implications of the idea in José Martí's "Nuestra América" (1891) that what is good or true depends on who we are—and ends by considering the political stakes and logical consequences involved in both the affirmation of identity and the repudiation of the universal in the present. This book challenges a series of widely held theoretical positions within Latin American literary and cultural studies—in particular, the idea that cultural practices can be logically justified on the grounds that they are ours; the repudiation of authorial intention and the notion that a reader's experience and participation are relevant to a text's meaning; the notion that we can somehow remember historical events that we never experienced; and finally, the claim that the celebration of cultural difference is a form of resistance to neoliberalism. What these seemingly disparate claims all share is the desire to sidestep the universality that is intrinsic to all beliefs.

It is a commonplace to claim that there are many equally valid truths and that different beliefs, instead of being true or false, are merely the product of different worldviews, epistemologies, epistemic systems, cultures, and subject positions.[5] Yet even those who make this claim, whenever they have disagreements, must nonetheless think their beliefs possess a truth that transcends particulars.[6] Otherwise, disagreement would be impossible. To put this a different way: we often refer to our beliefs as "subjective," but in order to disagree with others, we must think that the truth of our beliefs transcends our subject position. Otherwise, we would not be able to disagree. Disagreement thus reveals a simple truism about the nature of beliefs: to believe something is to believe that it is universally true.[7]

Nevertheless, universalism is commonly viewed not as an inescapable fact about our beliefs but rather as something to be challenged and refuted. Étienne Balibar, for example, ties universalism to racism, and argues that it undergirds "the domination of some cultures on others," a process that "works effectively *only* if those who carry them out [acts of domination] actually *believe* in their legitimacy and, indeed, in their truth, or in their being grounded in true doctrines."[8] Thus, he argues, universalism is merely the logical foundation for racist, discriminatory, and imperialist practices. However, Balibar's denunciation of racism, sexism, and imperialism is *already* profoundly universalist, and it depends on its "being grounded in true doctrines" even though it undoubtedly emerges from a cultural and historical particular (not all cultures, for example, have condemned racism). If we recognize that racism and sexism have been, and unfortunately continue to be, indisputably part of the culture of many people, antiracism and antisexism will always imply the imposition of "some cultures on others." But as long as we are committed to eradicating racism and sexism, it is hard to see why we should think this is a bad thing.[9]

However, the recent work of theorists such as Ernesto Laclau and Slavoj Žižek has, in different ways, offered warnings about the political limitations of particularism and called for a return to universalism. Laclau, for example, has argued that now "we have an increasing proliferation of [. . .] particularistic demands that create the potential—but only the potential—for more expanded chains of equivalence than in the past and, as a result, the possibility of more democratic societies."[10] However, Laclau notes, "we are living at a time in which the great emancipatory narratives of the past are in sharp decline, and as a result [. . .] there are no easily available universalizing discourses which could perform the equivalential function" (209). Therefore, the task of the Left, argues Laclau, is "the construction of language providing that element of universality which makes possible the establishment of equivalential links" (209).

Laclau is right when he argues that the rejection of "universalism in toto as the particular content of the West [. . .] can only lead to a political blind alley."[11] But ultimately Laclau sees universalism as a worthy aspiration that can never be achieved: universalism, he writes, "is incommensurable with any particularity yet cannot exist apart from the particular" (90). Universalism for Laclau is therefore an "impossible task that makes democratic interaction achievable" (90). But the universal is not a "task" that is achieved after everyone agrees; instead, it is what allows us to disagree in the here and now. Moreover, it does not bear the kind of complex relation to the particular that Laclau describes, and it is far from being an impossibility.

Stanley Fish, for example, has recently rehearsed many of the usual critiques of universalism, conceding not only that "our convictions cannot be grounded in any independent source of authority," but also that we will never be able to "settle the question of which epistemic system is correct" from outside our epistemic system.[12] Nevertheless, Fish argues, the "unavailability of independent grounds—of foundations that are general and universal rather than local and contextual—is fraught with no implications at all."[13] In other words, once we realize that our beliefs "are not underwritten by grounds independent of the complex of assumptions and experience from which they emerge," we also realize that our beliefs "are none the worse (or better) for that, because that same complex of assumptions and experience provides [us] with everything (knowledge, imperatives, confidence) promised by the independent grounds [we] will never find."[14] Rather than posit that any of this forecloses on the possibility of the universal, Fish claims that rationality is not "a single thing whose protocols can be recognized and accepted by persons of varying and opposing beliefs."[15] Therefore, he argues, disagreement is never between "the rational and the irrational" but rather "between opposing rationalities."[16]

Ultimately, I suggest that, far from being something anyone needs to return to, universalism is already something we are committed to inasmuch as we have beliefs, regardless of the particular, local reasons we invoke to justify them. For it is in the very act of invoking reasons to justify a belief in the first place that we both glimpse the universal and realize that our reasons for holding our beliefs are not merely "our" reasons but in fact the right reasons. Nevertheless, the replacement of the universally true with the locally true is often thought to be a prerequisite for the recovery and/or preservation of non-Western beliefs, epistemologies, identities, and forms of social organization. While such efforts are grounded in the important desire for alternatives to Western capitalist modernity, we do no favor to our beliefs or the beliefs of others when we strip them of the universal implications they intrinsically contain. As Susan Haack has argued, the rejection of the universal is profoundly "cynical," since if one gives up on the idea that one's beliefs are true, then "one would be obliged to adopt an attitude of cynicism towards them, to think of justification always in covert scare quotes."[17]

If the universal is neither an impossibility nor an aspiration, it is also neither the cosmopolitan nor the global. To be sure, discussions of the universal in Latin Americanist thought (which have, of course, their own long and complex history) have tended to equate the universal with the cosmopolitan and the foreign.[18] The frequently used terms "*literatura universal*" (universal literature) and "*historia universal*" (universal history) equate the universal with a kind of globality that is misleading. The argument of this book is not that the subject needs to be *everywhere* or *everyone* in order to be universal and make universal claims but rather that *anyone anywhere* who has a belief is already committed to its universality. Ángel Rama, for example, writes in *The Lettered City* (1984) of the ways that late nineteenth-century intellectuals sought to "reconcile the irresistible attractions of universalism with the maintenance of national traditions and the existing grid of social values."[19] Rama's understanding of the "attractions of universalism" as automatically opposed to "the existing grid of social values" is telling, for it incorrectly assumes that those same "social values" are not themselves universal values. It is as if, Rama seems to suggest, one must achieve what he calls a "lofty perspective," transcending one's particularity, to think that our beliefs and values are not just true, given who we are, but rather true, regardless of who we are. However, the desire to maintain our social values in the first place is rooted not in their being ours but rather in our belief that they are the true values—hence the desire to preserve them. To think that cosmopolitanism is a necessary prerequisite for the universal is just the other side of the anti-universalist coin, since it means thinking that the truth of our beliefs depends on the subject position we occupy—hence the desire to occupy a vast, cosmopolitan one.

Nevertheless, the argument in John Beverley's *Latinamericanism after 9/11* (2011) is that the urgent task facing the Left in Latin America is developing a renewed anti-universalism. What is needed, argues Beverley, is to recover "for the discourse of the Left the space of cultural dehierarchization ceded to the market and to neoliberalism."[20] Beverley's timely book acknowledges that neoliberal ideology has achieved cultural dehierarchization more effectively than any Left project, including Latin Americanism, meaning that the core commitment of Latin Americanism seems to be "complicit with precisely that which we want to resist" (21). However, Beverley urges a return to, rather than a departure from, the recurring assumptions of Latin American thought that are the subject of this book. I question, on the contrary, whether "cultural dehierarchization" should have ever been the basis for a discourse of the Left and argue that now, more than ever, it has no place in any politics of the Left.

Beverley affirms the importance of thinking that "there is no one standard for truth," so therefore "claims about truth are contextual: they have to do with how people construct different understandings of the world" (62). I argue that this implies a circularity, in which the only possible justification for our beliefs, since they are of "equal worth," is that they happen to be ours. This carries with it a problem: if beliefs are of equal worth, then there is no reason to change them, and changing them begins to seem like an act of self-betrayal. Like Beverley, I believe that Latin America carries within it the hope for "an alternative future" (18). However, that future will not be reached when truths from Latin America are rendered just as good as any others and better *only for us*. Instead, an alternative future will be achieved when truths from Latin America are given a framework by Latin Americanism that allows them to be understood as contending with those of other ideologies rather than merely as markers of identitarian difference.

The arguments in *The Limits of Identity* build on the work of philosophers and theorists such as Paul Boghossian, Stanley Fish, and especially Walter Benn Michaels. Michaels's work—especially *Our America: Nativism, Modernism, and Pluralism* (1995) and *The Shape of the Signifier: 1967 to the End of History* (2004)—deals primarily with the political and theoretical impasses of identity in the United States, but the implications of his arguments concerning identity and difference need not end there. The point of departure for the arguments in this book is what Abraham Acosta has recently identified as a "crisis of resistance" due to the fact that "predominant theories of Latin American culture have been and continue to be insufficiently conceived to account for the critical and heterogeneous realities of modernization in the region."[21] At the same time, this book contributes to a growing turn in the field defined in part by the pathbreaking work of Eugenio Di Stefano and Emilio Sauri, which holds that the theoretical commitment to the "different positions individual and collective subjects assume within society" produces a version of politics that "renders the structure of exploitation itself a secondary, if not altogether irrelevant concern."[22] Moreover, Di Stefano and Sauri argue that the commitment to the "primacy of the subject's position" and the "emphasis on experience" in recent Latin American literary and cultural studies ultimately "functions to make the cause of that experience—capitalist economic relations—tangential at best, irrelevant at worst."[23]

Chapter 1 provides an account of the historical and ideological conditions that gave rise to anti-universalism and the commitment to identity in nineteenth-century Latin America. My main focus, however, is on Martí's foundational essay, "Nuestra América," which contains the logic of what became the dominant modes of Latin American cultural normativity in the twentieth century. Indeed, as Alberto Moreiras has argued, the essential preoccupation of Latin Americanism has been "preserving, no matter in how contradictory or tense [a] manner, an idea of Latin America as the repository of a cultural difference that would resist assimilation by Eurocentric modernity."[24] Even though "Nuestra América" famously repudiates biological race and champions what Martí calls "the universal identity of man," it also prescribes a set of beliefs and practices that Martí insists should not be understood as better for everyone, but rather only better *for Latin Americans*.[25] If the cornerstone of biological race-thinking is the idea that what we do is a function of who we are, Martí replaces that with the notion that what we do should be a reflection who we are. I argue that, far from offering a post-racial vision, Martí's concept of culture reinstates the concept of race that he repudiates. Martí's "Nuestra América" thus signals neither the end of race nor the emergence of post-racialism. Although most theoretical accounts of neo-racism, such as Étienne Balibar's, insist that universalism and "the theme of hierarchy" are always present beneath the surface of neo-racisms, I argue that it is precisely the commitment to anti-universalism and the rejection of the hierarchical that enable the most pervasive forms of neo-racism.[26] What is at stake is whether any anti-universalist cultural project can escape a dependence on biological race.

In chapter 2 I explore how José Enrique Rodó's *Ariel* (1900) recognizes both the emancipatory power and the identitarian indifference of beliefs. *Ariel* was published at a time when positivist-influenced writing about Latin America's social and political problems—such as César Zumeta's *Continente enfermo* (1899)—saw the region as a sick body troubled by its physical features (the racialized bodies of its inhabitants or the deterministic nature of its natural environment). But instead of casting Latin America as defined by the instincts of racial others or governed by its physical reality, Rodó suggests that Latin America is in fact the heir to the best and highest ideals of Western civilization. The essence of Latin America, Rodó implies, is to be found in its ideals. However, inasmuch as one of Rodó's aims was to establish and secure a distinctive regional identity, this creates a problem. I argue that this causes *Ariel* to reverse its commitment to the disembodied ideals that it is best known for advancing in favor of notions of materiality and the body that could secure difference in a way that beliefs and ideals never can. I close with a discussion of Rodolfo Kusch's *Indigenous and Popular Thinking in América* (1970), a text that, albeit in different ways and on different terms, attempts to protect difference from disagreement.

Chapter 3 focuses on the emergence of anti-universalist accounts of what a text means. I read Jorge Luis Borges's "Pierre Menard, Author of the *Quixote*" (1939) as a story that, contrary to what is often said, underscores the universalism of textual meaning. In turn, "Pierre Menard" helps make clear what, beginning in the 1960s, many Latin American critics and theorists began trying to overcome—namely, the fact that what a text means has nothing to do with the reader's identity or experience. This explains the identitarian stakes of a wide range of efforts to replace questions of meaning with descriptions of a text's effects on readers. Indeed, as Roberto Fernández Retamar wrote in 1975, while the act of looking at the formal properties of a text or producing a "description of a literary work's structures" is perhaps "interesting," such analysis fails to deal with what he thinks matters.[27] For Fernández Retamar, what matters is a text's "functional instrumentality," which is really to say, its effects on readers.[28] I argue that what is at stake for Fernández Retamar and others is the desire to overcome meaning's universality by imagining how the identity of the reader, rather than the intention of the author, is what matters about a text.

In chapter 4 I trace the rise, beginning in the 1980s, of the idea that the historical past in Latin America is something that can—and should—be remembered. In an analysis of texts ranging from Eduardo Galeano's *Memory of Fire* (1982–1986) to Guillermo Bonfil Batalla's *México profundo* (1987) and Carmen Boullosa's *Cielos de la tierra* (1997), I explore how the Latin Americanist imperative to *practice* a given culture was replaced with the imperative to *remember* it. At the same time, there emerged an anti-universalist negation of historical truth that undermined the difference between knowledge and experience. Thus, I argue that this new account of the relationship between history and memory sought to make history a source for identitarian difference, which was a response to growing uncertainty about the persistence of difference in the face of neoliberal globalization. For example, if in *Forjando patria* (1916), one of the founding texts of Mexican *indigenismo* and revolutionary nationalism, Manuel Gamio could claim that "75 percent" of the population of Latin America was "composed of men of [. . .] indigenous language, and indigenous civilization," in 2001 Néstor García Canclini argued that the "aesthetic taste" of Mexicans was overwhelmingly informed by U.S. television and film, which constituted 60 to 85 percent of all media consumption in the country.[29] Thus, by imagining difference in the past as memory, history could take up the identitarian work once performed by culture and beliefs in the present. I argue not only that the turn to memory did the work of culture but also that it offered a model of identitarian difference complicit with the growth of neoliberal global consumer and labor markets.

This book, however, is not primarily a *history* of identity and anti-universalism in Latin American thought. There is already an impressive body of work that has taken on that task, and while there is perhaps more to be done, that is not the goal of this book.[30] Instead, *The Limits of Identity* makes an argument about Latin Americanism—namely, that although its origins can be located in an attempt to repudiate the universalization of a Eurocentric modernity, it ultimately established itself as a repudiation not of a bad universal but of universality writ large, thus becoming as hostile to true beliefs as it is to false ones. As such,

Latin Americanism not only blunts the force of the very beliefs and values it set out to affirm but also implicates itself in many of the same discourses that it sought to repudiate.

In the coda I discuss one of the most recent interventions into Latin American literary and cultural studies, John Beverley's *Latinamericanism after 9/11*. Beverley's book is significant for the way that it both concedes the exhaustion of Latin Americanist ideologies and at the same time calls for a retrenchment in them. At the heart of what he proposes for a new Latin Americanism is a renewed commitment to identity and anti-universalism. However, I argue that just the opposite is needed, pointing toward the possibility of a new Latin Americanism, but one no longer concerned with identitarian difference qua difference, and no longer resting on anti-universalist grounds.

CHAPTER ONE

Culture

THE IMPORTANCE OF JOSÉ MARTÍ'S "NUESTRA AMÉ-
rica" (1891)—arguably the most canonical Latin American
essay—rests on the text's two central commitments: the repudiation of
biological race and the celebration of Latin American cultural difference. It is usually thought that these two commitments are compati-
ble, but just the opposite is true, even though "Nuestra América" appears to repudiate race definitively and decisively. Martí declares that
"there are no races" and then dismisses the idea of race as the business
of "sickly, lamp-lit minds."[1] Furthermore, he argues, "in the justice of
nature" there is only "the universal identity of man" (296).

In other texts by Martí that deal not with the regional issues ad-
dressed in "Nuestra América" but with the issue of Cuban nationalism to which he devoted his life, we can find similarly purposeful re-
pudiations of race. In "My Race" (1893), for example, Martí writes that
"anything that divides men from each other, that separates them, sin-
gles them out, or hems them in, is a sin against humanity" (318).[2] Those
who believe that a "virus" exists in the "black man," he argues, are per-
petuating a "sin against humanity" (318–319). He then chides "the black
man who trumpets his race" because he perpetuates "a sin against humanity" as much as the "white man who, by reason of his race, believes
himself superior to the black man" (318–319).

"Nuestra América" originated from Martí's belief that the people of
the United States exhibited "characteristics" such as "ideas and habits
of expansion, acquisition, vanity, and greed" that were becoming a "serious threat to the neighboring, isolated and weak lands that the strong
country declares to be perishable and inferior" (296). Martí nevertheless insists that "we must not [. . .] impute some lethal congenital wick-

edness to the continent's light-skinned nation simply because it does not speak our language or share our view of what home life should be or resemble us in its political failings" (296). Martí refuses to see the differences between Latin Americans and North Americans—that is, their respective "characteristics," "ideas," and "habits"—as functions of anything "congenital," and he thus replaces race with a concept of culture. That is to say, if our "characteristics," "ideas," and "habits" are not functions of our racial identity (because there is no such thing as race), then they must be constituents of our cultural identity.

However, Martí's concept of culture ultimately depends on the concept of race that he repudiates. To be sure, Martí repudiates race and insists that our practices and beliefs have no grounding in our heredity; in so doing, Martí breaks the link between culture and race that is at the heart of racialism.[3] But at the same time, Martí claims that Latin Americans can betray, deny, or lose their culture—a claim that restores the link between race and culture that was severed by his repudiation of race. Martí's concept of culture is striking and original not because it eschews race during a time when the idea of race held powerful sway on Latin American politics and thought but because it does the work of race in new and hidden ways. Martí wrote "Nuestra América" barely five years after the end of slavery in Cuba, and in light of that fact, it is not remarkable that he would fail to abandon race. What is remarkable is that his ideas about culture have yet to be abandoned by Latin Americanist thought more than a century later.

The authority of "Nuestra América" within Latin Americanist thought is readily apparent in texts such as "Caliban: Notes Toward a Discussion of Culture in Our America," Roberto Fernández Retamar's influential essay from 1971.[4] More recently, some of the most prominent Latin Americanist scholars and theorists have celebrated Martí's ideas and underlined their enduring relevance to the present. Walter Mignolo, for example, describes Martí as "a postcolonial Caribbean intellectual, in today's sense of 'postcolonial,'" and Fernando Coronil lists Martí—alongside Stuart Hall—among those who influenced his work.[5]

"Nuestra América" has been mobilized as both a forerunner of South Asian postcolonial theory and an organic Latin American theoretical alternative to it, and it has served as a model for what José David Saldívar calls "comparative cultural studies."[6] Indeed, "Nuestra América" is repeatedly held up as a fresh, new roadmap for the Latin American future or as an unfinished project whose state of unfinishedness defines the present tasks of Latin Americanism. In "Caliban," Fernández Retamar insists that Martí's "true place was the future and, for the moment, this era of ours, which simply cannot be understood without a thorough knowledge of his work."[7] Here we can see the contradictory ways in which "Nuestra América" tends to be read. In essence, readings of "Nuestra América" are simultaneously historicist and dehistoricizing: on the one hand, the assumption is that "Nuestra América" acquires its meaning and authority as a challenge to the racist, imperialist, and Eurocentric discourses that surrounded it in the late nineteenth century; on the other hand, "Nuestra América" is thought to be uncontaminated by the same discourses that it is celebrated for opposing.[8] Thus, as long as the essay is not implicated in the history from which it emerged, the reassertion of its ideas seems less like an orthodoxy and more like a radical innovation.[9] What is ultimately at stake in a critique of "Nuestra América," however, is not only the sanctified status of a nineteenth-century essay but also the body of Latin Americanist thought that continues to adhere to its main claims.

Martí's views on race and culture were born from a series of related Latin American problems: the menace of U.S. political and economic hegemony, the continued authority of imported ideas and cultural norms, and widely held notions of Latin American inferiority. Martí's response to these problems was conditioned by the politics of race in nineteenth-century Cuban nationalism. In fact, the phrase "nuestra América" implicitly took on these problems: it not only implied a demarcation between two distinct Americas but also set aside the question of inferiority and superiority in favor of the question of what is and is not ours. As Martí wrote in 1894, "on the one hand, there is our America, [. . .] and on the other hand, there is the America that is not ours," thereby emphasizing that the only relevant fact about "our America" is that it is "ours."[10]

"Nuestra América" was written on the heels of Martí's attendance at the First International Conference of American States in Washington, D.C. (the "Pan-American Conference"), from October 1889 to April 1890, which had been organized by U.S. Secretary of State James G. Blaine.[11] Officially, the agenda for the Pan-American Conference dealt with issues of trade, currency, and the arbitration of disputes between nations, but Martí believed that the conference was merely a pretext for the economic, political, and cultural domination of Latin American nations by the United States.[12] In his first report on the conference for the Buenos Aires newspaper *La Nación* on November 2, 1889, Martí declared that "the powerful United States, with its surplus of goods" was "determined to extend its dominion over Latin America" (6:46). Having seen the "brazen beginnings of an era of U.S. domination over all the nations of the Americas," Martí called the United States a "scornful Juggernaut that advances triumphantly [. . .] squashing the heads of its servants" (6:53–54). The task facing Latin America, he concluded, was to "declare a second independence" by issuing a "strong and unanimous" response to the imperial designs of the United States (6:46).

In calling for a "second independence," Martí's point was that Latin America's independence movements had not eliminated intellectual, cultural, political, and economic dependence. Latin American independence rested—at least rhetorically—on assumptions about the universal translatability and applicability of Enlightenment liberalism.[13] Translations of Thomas Paine, John Adams, Thomas Jefferson, George Washington, and the U.S. Constitution and Declaration of Independence circulated widely among elites.[14] Prominent intellectuals and statesmen from that period, such as Juan Pablo Viscardo y Guzmán, Antonio Nariño, Fray Servando Teresa de Mier, Francisco de Miranda, and Manuel Belgrano, looked to the United States in particular as an example for Latin America's political and military struggles for independence. Miranda, for example, wrote in 1799 that they had "two great examples" before their eyes: "the American Revolution and the French"; he argued that they should "imitate [. . .] the former, trying to avoid with as much care as possible the disastrous effects of the latter."[15] Roughly five years earlier, during his trial on charges of having translated and distributed copies of France's Declaration of the Rights of Man, Antonio Nariño declared that "when our colonies shall have grown in population and industry, they, too, will want to be independent sovereign states, following the example of their Northern Neighbors."[16]

Many of the key texts produced during the struggles for independence proclaimed both the universality of the political models offered by the United States and France and the readiness of Latin Americans to duplicate them. Latin American *independentistas* thus often sought to erase the idea of Latin American difference because the content of that difference was thought to be identical to an undesirable colonial situation. In "An Open Letter to América" (1799), for example, Viscardo y Guzmán invoked "self-evident principles" to argue that Spanish colonial authorities had stripped American subjects of their "natural rights," the preservation of which, he argued, is undoubtedly the "foundation stone of every human society."[17] The "dependence on Spain must end," he proclaimed, adding that American subjects have the right to "defend the inalienable rights given by our Creator."[18] One of Viscardo's objectives was correcting the misleading impression created by the writings of European Enlightenment intellectuals such as Guillaume-Thomas Raynal, William Robertson, and Antonio de Ulloa, whose claims about the inferiority of New World subjects were used to support arguments against independence.[19] Viscardo, in other words, had to challenge the idea of Latin American difference to insert Latin America into a framework of universal rights that could in turn underpin its demands for self-governance.

The debate over the real political and intellectual origins of Latin American independence is less relevant to the question of "Nuestra América" than the ubiquity of the rhetoric of U.S. exemplarity, which assumed the superiority and universal applicability of North American ideas and political models.[20] After the wars of independence, all of that gave way to a political and cultural logic in which, as Martí put it in "Nuestra América," there was "too much imitation" (294).[21] This logic of imitation is reflected in the fact that the constitutions of Venezuela (1811), Mexico (1824), the Central American Federation (1825), and Argentina (1826) were directly modeled on the U.S. Constitution; federalism, judicial review, and even electoral colleges were widely embraced and implemented.[22] In the 1880s, Domingo Faustino Sarmiento had somewhat infamously declared, "Let us be the United States," thereby illustrating the logic that permeated Latin American politics and thought in the nineteenth century.[23]

The contradiction of this period, as it has been traditionally understood, is that the European and North American ideas that underpinned Latin America's political independence from Spain also guaranteed its cultural and intellectual dependence on Europe and the United States. In the words of Leopoldo Zea, the trouble was that "the same philosophy that [. . .] had presented itself as a philosophy of liberation became a philosophy of domination that justified the interests of the centers of power from which it originated."[24] Martí is often cast as the first Latin American intellectual to critique European and North American modernity or affirm Latin American cultural difference as a form of resistance to it.[25] In truth, however, by the middle of the nineteenth century, in the wake of events such as the annexation of Texas by the United States in 1845, the U.S. invasion of Mexico in 1846, William Walker's invasion of Nicaragua in 1855, and France's invasion of Mexico in 1861, many Latin American intellectuals began to critique the ideas and values originating in the same nations—in particular the United States—that had imperial designs on the region.[26] This critical attitude can be seen in texts such as Francisco Bilbao's "El congreso normal americano" (1856), as well as in José María Torres Caicedo's *Unión Latino-Americana* (1865), which espouses a concept of regional unity that anticipates Martí's "Nuestra América."[27]

Latin American independence had been achieved during a time when there was widespread faith in the power of written laws based on universal, abstract principles to guarantee good government, individual liberty, and social order.[28] Indeed, as George Athan Billias points out, liberal elites in Latin America believed that the success of the United States "resulted from its political and constitutional institutions and not necessarily from the character of its people."[29] But the fact that the establishment of liberal, republican political institutions was followed by *caudillismo* and political unrest brought about a questioning of the universality of political theories, although not necessarily a questioning of the universality that enabled notions of European or North American superiority. If North American and European political theories no longer appeared to be applicable to every country, then one conclusion was that people were not the same everywhere.

As a result, there was a growing sense that imported ideas and models had caused the region's political turmoil: as Esteban Echeverría put it, "to appeal to the authority of European thinkers is to introduce anarchy, confusion, and mayhem into the answers to our questions," and moreover, "it is to confess our inability to understand what we are."[30] Beginning in the 1860s, the idea that the region's problems would be solved by confronting and fully understanding national and regional particularities was consolidated around the rise of positivism.[31] As Zea has argued, the Latin American positivists "had no interest in a liberalism that believed in the magical power of words and assumed that it was enough to declare oneself a liberal and a democrat in order to convert one's country into liberal democracies such as those that emerged in Europe and the United States."[32] Thus, in a broad sense, positivism brought about a focus on Latin American identity and difference, albeit in negative terms. It is worth recalling that this is at least how José Enrique Rodó understood positivism's lasting influence over his generation: "the rite of passage through positivism," he wrote in *El mirador de Próspero* (1913), "left with us [. . .] its powerful concept of relativism [and] a skepticism regarding absolute claims."[33]

But even though positivism spurred the study of Latin American particularity, it imbued Latin American inferiority with the authority of European scientism. In positivist accounts of Latin America, theories of racial inferiority predominated, and the growing sense among many intellectuals was that the success of the United States could be attributed to the fact that it was a nation of Anglo-Saxon immigrants in which blacks and indigenous people had been marginalized.[34] This attitude, dominant even during the decades that followed the publication of "Nuestra América," can be found in Sarmiento's *Conflicto y armonías de las razas en América* (1883), as well as in texts such as Carlos Octavio Bunge's *Nuestra América* (1903), Francisco Carrera y Justiz's *La intervención y su política* (1906), Alcides Arguedas's *Pueblo enfermo* (1909), José Ingenieros's *Sociología argentina* (1931), and Ezequiel Martínez Estrada's *Radiografía de la pampa* (1933). Less than a decade after Martí's "Nuestra América," for example, Bunge's *Nuestra América* argued that the "lack of moral sense" among "American racial hybrids" explained why the "characteristic phenomena of Spanish-American political economy" are "rulers of blood and pillage."[35]

In "Nuestra América," Martí correctly believed that notions of European and North American racial superiority had enabled the overvaluing of what he calls "imported forms and ideas" (292), which in turn included, by the end of the nineteenth century, a range of supposedly scientific racial theories that reified existing assumptions about the inferiority of blacks, Indians, mestizos, and mulattoes.[36] As Aline Helg points out, in the last quarter of the nineteenth century, many Latin American elites—influenced by positivism, social Darwinism, geographical determinism, and European racial theories—attributed "civil wars and the failure of postindependence democratic institutions" to the "racial inferiority of Latin America."[37] In the case of Cuba, race posed a somewhat different problem, given that race and racial distinctions had been one of the main obstacles to the island's independence.

While Martí's claim that "there are no races" was possibly a manifestation of his putative commitment to antiracism, it was undoubtedly a calculated political gesture in the context of the national and regional projects he was advancing.[38] In the case of Latin America in general, Martí saw race as an impediment to regional solidarity and the legitimation of Latin American identity. In the case of Cuba, Martí saw race as an obstacle to interracial political alliances for independence. The repudiation of race was necessary for Martí because Cuba's struggle for independence had been hampered by the failure to reconcile the reality of a multiracial population with the idea of a Cuban nation. Advocates of colonialism had argued that Cuba's black population made an independent, sovereign Cuba impossible, or if possible, undesirable for whites. Furthermore, the fact of Cuba's substantial mixed-race and black population, as Alejandro de la Fuente notes, was routinely invoked to support arguments against the idea of a Cuban nation by

Creole whites in Cuba as well as by North American and other foreign authorities.[39]

At least until around 1868, or the beginning of the Ten Years' War (1868–1878), Creole elites seemed willing to settle for Spanish rule (or annexation to the United States) because they believed colonial status protected them from a Haitian-style slave rebellion. In fact, Spanish colonial authorities systematically exploited Creoles' fear of slave rebellion and race war after the Haitian Revolution, even possibly falsifying, as Hugh Thomas suggests, the census of 1792, the first to demonstrate a black majority population in Cuba.[40] Louis Pérez argues that by the time Cuba's black population became a majority, "nothing so preyed on creole consciousness [. . .] as the specter of slave rebellion and race war."[41] Additionally, he argues, since "slave rebellions during the nineteenth century confirmed creoles' worse fears," their "swift repression by the Spanish army provided creoles with comforting reassurance that their confidence in the efficacy of *peninsular* arms had not been misplaced."[42] The Ten Years' War marked a change in that way of thinking, as Creole elites offered tenuous support for independence. However, as Lillian Guerra has shown, this support largely vanished when Creoles realized the role, power, and number of blacks in the rebel army, who cast "abolition as the twin goal of independence" and were radicalizing the "social vision" of the independence movement.[43] In other words, just as white racial fears delayed Cuba's independence movement, they accounted for the failure of the Ten Years' War, Cuba's fractious first armed struggle for national sovereignty. Recognizing that Cuba's independence movement could succeed only with racial "unity" and faced with the racial fears that had impeded unity, Martí explicitly and repeatedly tried to allay fears of race war (345). "There will never be a race war in Cuba," he wrote in "My Race" (320). But he went further in "Nuestra América," trying to eliminate racial fears by repudiating the idea of race on which those fears were based: "there are no races," he declared (295).

Martí's new language of national unity—in which "'Cuban' means more than white, more than mulatto, more than Negro" (319)—replaces the terms on which the question of Cuba's racial composition might be posed with an all-inclusive *cubanidad* based not on identity (black or white or mulatto) but on ideology (what one believes). By making *cubanidad* a matter of ideology, he aimed to check the identitarian allegiances that had impeded a unified multiracial Cuban independence movement. Ada Ferrer has shown that this strategy worked: by the 1890s, official documents "routinely failed to record any information regarding individuals' racial identification."[44] In fact, she notes, the "list of roughly forty thousand members of the rebel army who survived the final war carefully recorded for each soldier" every piece of information except his race.[45] According to Ferrer, all of this points to the success of the "color-blind" project of those, like Martí, who repeatedly insisted that the "constant allusion to a man's skin color should cease."[46]

In addition to repudiating the idea of different biologically constituted races—a concept that had been problematic for Cuban *independentista* projects—Martí set out to redefine the nature of the conflict between nationalist insurgents and those opposed to the project of a Cuban nation. In a race war, the conflict is fundamentally identitarian: the question of which side we are on in a race war is answered by referring to who we are. Martí sought to transform the conflict into one of ideologies rather than identities, so that the identitarian differences between white and black *independentistas* could be replaced with political unity based on shared beliefs. That is why Martí insists that the black man should want freedom and independence based not on being black but rather on a commitment to the universal ideals of independence and freedom.[47] Martí makes difference identical to disagreement so that "political parties" replace "the varying colors of men" as the grounds for "unity" or "opposition" (320).

In redefining the struggle for independence as a conflict of ideologies and not of identities, Martí did more than make race irrelevant; he made identity irrelevant *tout court*. By definition, ideological conflict makes identity irrelevant, since it is only when we believe that something is true not only for us, given who we are, but also for everyone, whoever they are, that there can be an ideological conflict in the first place. Some might object to this claim on the grounds that our positions in an ideological conflict are already determined by our identity; the beliefs we have are the product, in some form or another, of our experience and identity. According to that line of argument, ideological conflicts are reducible to the difference between the identities that produced the conflicting beliefs. However, ideological conflict transcends identity because it depends on thinking that the truth of our beliefs extends beyond our identity. If we really thought that our beliefs are only true given who we are, or that having a belief makes it true for the believer, then we could never have disagreements.[48]

Martí's desire to see difference as disagreement makes not only race but also any form of identity irrelevant, and it also offers a glimpse of what a truly post-identitarian politics actually looks like. After all, it was identity that had prevented the success of a multiracial independence movement, and it was also identity that had been the basis for claims by the United States and other nations that Cubans were unfit to govern themselves. In place of thinking that what matters is who we are, Martí thinks that what matters is what we believe. When he writes that Cuban means "more than white" or "more than Negro," he cannot really mean "more," since he understands "Negro" and "white" to be meaningless categories—instead, he means that Cuban is a category that, because it is based only on beliefs, transcends any and all particulars (319). Martí's claim that differences between men are differences only between "political parties" renders not only the body but also any form of identity irrelevant to the (exclusively ideological) difference that matters to Martí (320).

Martí's replacement of identity with ideology erases the identitarian barriers that had been so deeply problematic to the project of Cuban nationalism. Making difference identical to disagreement allows Martí not only to transcend conflicts based on identitarian grounds but also to transcend identity. Cuban unity, he argues, derives only from shared beliefs, not shared identities, and to be Cuban, he suggests elsewhere, is to believe in "liberty" and reject "tyranny" (264). Indeed, the identitarian differences among the leaders of Cuba's independence movement—which included Carlos Roloff, a Polish Jew; Antonio Maceo, the mulatto son of a Venezuelan; and Horatio Rubens, a North American attorney—is evidence of the identitarian transcendence made possible by the replacement of identity with ideology.

It is the idea that ideological affinities trump identitarian ones that Martí emphasizes in his reply to an article that appeared in the *New York Evening Post* on March 21, 1889. In that article, a North American writer argued that "native Cubans" were characterized by "effeminacy and a distaste for exertion which amounts really to disease" (262). Moreover, the author stated, Cubans "are helpless, idle, of defective morals, and unfitted by nature and experience for discharging the obligations of citizenship in a great and free republic" (262). In his letter to the editor on March 23, Martí affirms the similarities between Cubans and North Americans in the light of their shared beliefs and values. In New York, argues Martí, Cubans "are directors of prominent banks, substantial merchants, popular brokers, clerks of recognized ability, physicians with a large practice, engineers of world-wide repute, electricians, journalists, tradesmen, cigarmakers" (265). Moreover, he adds, Cubans "have fought like men" (264) and share with North Americans a desire for "freedom from religious intolerance" and faith in the "laws and processes of liberty" (266). The task for Martí's nationalism, in other words, was dismantling the concept of Cuban difference by positing the universality of *cubanidad* based on ideology: to be Cuban is merely to believe in "liberty" and fight against "tyranny" (264). Cubans, Martí declares, "have made of the heroes of [the United States] their own heroes" (264).

Martí's vision of a disembodied *cubanidad* based on ideology dismantled the identitarian roadblocks to Cuban independence. It negated the difference between blacks and whites in Cuba but also erased the difference between Cubans and others that had been invoked against the cause of Cuban independence. The idea of *cubanidad* based only on ideology, however, solved one problem and created another—at least for Martí. He was, after all, both a regionalist and a nationalist, and the idea that what binds people together is ideology is not enough to hold a nation or region together—in fact, it is inimical to nationalism and regionalism. The trouble with ideology, if you are Martí, is that beliefs are intrinsically universal: to believe something is to believe that it is true for everyone. If we think that what makes someone a member of our nation or region is his or her beliefs, then we must think that anyone who shares our beliefs is a member of our nation or region. We must also think that those who do not hold our beliefs should start holding them. In other words, the notion of national or regional distinctiveness based on ideology logically entails an indifference to the preservation of national and regional distinctiveness. If *cubanidad* is to be understood in terms of shared beliefs, then *cubanidad* becomes just another name for the universally true. The powerful universalism that made possible the Cuban nation—by undergirding its appeals for independence and negating the importance of the identitarian differences that had impeded it—was thus always in tension with the nationalist project for which it was invoked. The same can be said for the regionalist project of "Nuestra América," where Martí undoes the universalism he envisions and returns to the idea of race he repudiates.

The reasons for this return can be seen in the second poem from Martí's *Versos sencillos* (1891). Like "Nuestra América," *Versos sencillos* grew out of Martí's experience at the Pan-American Conference: in the prologue, he writes that "these verses grew from my heart" in an "anguished winter when, out of ignorance, blind faith, fear, or mere politeness, the peoples of Latin America gathered in Washington beneath the fearsome eagle" (270). Martí begins the second poem in the book by declaring, "I know of Egypt and Niger, / Of Persia and Xenophon, no less, / But more than these I prefer / The fresh mountain air's caress."[49]

Cathy Jrade has pointed out that the contrast between "I know" and "I prefer" has "epistemological implications" and "metaphoric associations related to nationhood and national identity."[50] However, the contrast between what Jrade calls different "ways of knowing" is a distinction between knowledge and something that is different from knowledge—namely, experience. Martí knows "Egypt and Niger," but he feels the "mountain air's caress." In the second stanza, Martí also states a preference for experience over knowledge: "I know the ancient histories / Of man and his struggles for power, / But I prefer the buzzing bees / That hover round the bellflower."[51] Beyond merely preferring the intensely local—"the buzzing bees" and "the mountain air's caress"—Martí is protecting local difference from the universalism implied by knowledge. For the things he embraces about the local are in fact things that are registered bodily through sensory experience—the "buzzing" and the "caress." We have to have been to the Cuban *monte* to experience its "mountain air's caress," and we will each experience it differently. Whereas we can disagree about what counts as knowledge, we cannot disagree about how something makes us feel. Our experience of the "buzzing" and the "caress," unlike what we know, will be uniquely and irreducibly our own. The question of how we experience those things, unlike the question of what counts as knowledge, will be answered by referring to aspects of who we are. Herein lies the trouble with knowledge for Martí: it implies a universalism that is hostile to identity and difference, given that knowledge is a form of true belief. Affect and experience, on the other hand, are neither true nor false and have everything to do with who we are. Insofar as the bees' buzzing and the air's caress are registered sensorially, the uniqueness of how we experience them is fundamentally grounded in the uniqueness of who we are.

If Martí at first seems to argue that the differences between people are differences in belief, he ultimately argues that differences in belief are reducible to differences between people. Indeed, culture functions in "Nuestra América" not as a description of the things we do and believe that make us who we are but instead as a prescription of the things we *should* do and believe given who we are. As a result, the concept of culture becomes grounded in the very thing "Nuestra América" forcefully repudiates.[52]

Nevertheless, Martí's seemingly radical and monolithic repudiation of biological race has been celebrated for how it constitutes a major departure from the dominant, biologically determined accounts of race in nineteenth-century Latin America, or for how it anticipates the modern, social constructivist conception of race. Martí, who was raised in a slave-owning society during a period registering some of the most egregious instances of racism in recorded history, is often seen as a messianic figure who recognizes the injustices that stem from racial classification, purges himself of race and race-thinking, and calls on the world to do the same. In a 1941 speech in Havana on Martí and race dealing extensively with "Nuestra América," Fernando Ortiz declared that Martí purged "the racial concept of any genetic meaning of psychological nature and of social consequences."[53] Moreover, "Martí knows that 'our America' is not 'our race,' in any biological sense," and even though Martí happens to use the term "race," Ortiz argued, he does so "in its improper and vague but very current connotation, so as to attain a better understanding with his hearers or readers."[54] More recently, but in a similar vein, Lourdes Martínez-Echazábal celebrates the ways in which Martí's repudiation of race "places him in diametric opposition to other Latin American intellectuals and statesmen," and to support this claim she contrasts Martí's views on race in "Nuestra América" and "My Race" with those of José Ingenieros, who roughly twenty years later argued that "men of the colored race are unfit to exercise their civil capacity and ought not to be considered 'persons' in the juridical sense of the word."[55]

On its own, Martí's explicit denial of the biological category of race seems "prophetic" when compared to supposedly antiracist thinking in nineteenth- and twentieth-century Latin America, which often attempted to combat racism without repudiating the biological substance of racial categories.[56] Discussions of "Nuestra América" continue to advance the view of Martí as radically and wholly race transcendent, to such an extent that when Martí's position on race is critiqued, it is often on the grounds that it is *insufficiently* committed to race. Alejandra Bronfman, for example, claims that "Martí's race-transcendent ideology was nonetheless fraught with unresolved tensions between the need to overcome race and the impossibility of that goal: his strategy amounted to an attempt to overcome [race] by forgetting."[57] Bronfman's assumption is not only that Martí had completely moved beyond race but also that antiracism is incompatible with a prohibition on race-thinking. A similar position—exemplified by Ada Ferrer—holds that Martí's prohibition on race-thinking denies the terms on which a critique of racism would have to be made. According to Ferrer, the "repudiation of racism that encouraged black political activity at the end of the century" denied the "racial labels that allowed for that activity."[58] However, Ferrer's statement assumes that antiracism depends on race-thinking. Even if we believe that race-thinking is an effective weapon against racism, it does not make sense to understand the abolition of race-thinking as contradictory to an antiracist project. Race-thinking is what makes racism possible; if there were no such thing as race-thinking, there could be no such thing as racism.[59] It is not Martí's prohibition on all forms of race-thinking that conflicts with his antiracism but rather his cultural project, in which culture does the normative work of repudiated racial categories. Moreover, because culture entails an imperative for identity rather than merely a description of it, culture in "Nuestra América" does the identitarian work of race while seeming to abandon the identitarian ground of race.

Martí's cultural imperative stems from his fear that Latin Americans might "disown" their culture (289) by failing to be themselves: the "urgent duty of our America," Martí argues, "is to show herself as she is" (295). One of the central metaphors in Martí's essay involves "men born in America who are ashamed of the mother that raised them because she wears an Indian apron" (289).[60] The cultural project of "Nuestra América" as a whole can be understood as an attempt to undo this betrayal by aligning the practices of those who "desert" their indigenous mother with the practices of the indigenous mother herself (289). But if there is no such thing as race in Martí, and there is only culture, it logically follows that our culture is merely what we actually do and believe. In other words, an Indian apron would be part of our culture only if we actually wear an Indian apron.

Martí, however, understands culture as representing identity rather than constituting it; the Indian apron must be worn, he argues, because it is part of the culture of Latin Americans whether or not they actually wear it. Within this way of understanding culture, Latin Americans cannot refer to what they actually do and believe to explain who they are, since the things they actually do and believe are not necessarily part of their culture. Latin Americans must instead refer to an identity that is constituted by something other than their culture. In other words, the idea that our culture can be altogether different from what we do and believe requires culture to be located in race.

This should not be surprising, given that Martí's cultural project depends on a metaphor of biological fidelity: for Latin Americans to refuse to wear an Indian apron is for them to be "traitors," "ashamed" of their mother, and "cursing the bosom" from which they were born (289). If it is true, as David Lagmanovich suggests, that "metaphors *are* Martían thought" and "constitute the very substance of Martí's way of thinking," then a closer examination of Martí's biological metaphors would seem to suggest that "Nuestra América" is deeply implicated in race.[61] Indeed, only an appeal to biological race makes it possible to think that someone's choice not to do something could count as a betrayal. In other words, it is only race that can explain how the Indian apron has anything to do with those who do not wear it. The image in "Nuestra América" of the "men born in America," abandoning their sick mother because she wears the "Indian apron," contains the essence of Martí's cultural project.[62]

The point in Martí's Indian apron metaphor is not that Latin Americans should turn to the Indian mother because she offers a superior cultural model, but rather that Latin Americans should turn to themselves by turning to the Indian mother. The imperative to acknowledge the mother who wears an Indian apron depends entirely on a biological affinity with her. Just to be clear, Martí is not advancing classical racialism, in which there could never be a break between biology and culture, but neither is he advancing a post-racial account of culture, in which culture could only describe what we actually do and believe. Instead, Martí offers a new account of race, one in which the *can't* of classical racialism is replaced with a powerful *shouldn't*. In other words, the apparent racialism of Martí's culturalism is a new way of conceiving of race and not merely a camouflage for classical biological racialism. Martí's cultural "traitor" who rejects his mother's Indian apron is really a biological traitor, but the idea of biological treason is impossible in classical biological racialism, where the assumption is that cultural characteristics are determined by race.[63] In "Nuestra América," however, there is an implicit denial of the deterministic relationship between culture and biology: Martí acknowledges that Latin Americans can and sometimes do reject the Indian apron. This means not a wholesale rejection of that relationship, but rather a change in its nature. That is to say, Martí's idea of the cultural "traitor" creates a circuitous link between culture and biological race. In classical racialism, betrayal is impossible; without race, there is nothing to betray.

In "Nuestra América," Martí recognizes the power and implications of his own radical repudiation of race and racial identity—in other words, the logical consequences of his post-racialist conceptions of identity in which cultural identity can logically be nothing more than a description of what we do and believe. Martí's description of Latin America as a "dress ball" in which people disguise or betray their presumably "real" identity is a departure from racial determinism but not from racialism itself (293). It is the insistence on the idea that *something* is being disguised in Martí's "dress ball" metaphor that signals at least his unwillingness to abandon race and the body as the ground for identity. Without race, in other words, there is nothing to disguise. Or to extend Martí's metaphor, without race, we have an identity because of our clothes, not in spite of them. Martí sustains a commitment to race as the ground for identity, and this is what explains his repeated insistence that although Latin Americans can drive "Persian ponies" and drink "spilling champagne," such practices do not constitute their identity—an identity that is necessarily, in "Nuestra América," constituted by race (293).

What keeps Martí from abandoning race, or articulating a truly raceless culturalism, is his anti-universalism, which is a prerequisite for celebrating and preserving cultural difference.[64] Martí does not justify, or allow Latin Americans to justify, the cultural practices he prescribes by arguing that they are better than other practices; "Nuestra América" markedly rejects questions of cultural superiority and inferiority. Martí's anti-universalist rhetoric in "Nuestra América"—his claims that the "European university must yield to the American university" (291), that governments in Spanish America must be the products of "natural elements" grounded in "strategy" and not in principled abstractions, or that no "Yankee or European book" furnishes "the key to the Hispanoamerican enigma" (294)—are, to be sure, continuous with a major strain in nineteenth-century Latin American thought. In Simón Bolívar's "Angostura Address" (1819), for example, we already have the idea that "the laws of one nation" are not "applicable to another" because they "must take into account [. . .] its location [. . .] and the way of life of its people."[65] Bolívar implores the Venezuelan congress to seek out political truths that are local and establish a form of government "appropriate to their means, their spirit, and their circumstances" (47). The "code we should consult," writes Bolívar, is "not the one written for Washington" but rather the one that derives from "the physical aspect of the country, its climate, the nature of its terrain, its location, size, and the way of life of its people" (37).

But Martí's famous lines—"Make wine from plantains; it may be sour, but it is our wine!" (294)—radically sidestep the question of our America's value and affirm that our attachment to our America should be based only on the fact that it is ours. Latin Americans should feel "pride" in their "suffering republics" not because they are better but because they are ours (289). What Martí refers to as "natural elements" are preferable to things that are "imported" only on the grounds that they are ours. "Our own Greece," he wrote, "is preferable to the Greece that is not ours" (291).

The point is that Latin Americans should *not*, in fact, think that their culture is superior to other cultures. For to believe that the Indian apron is better than "English trousers" would mean wanting those who wear English trousers to wear the Indian apron (293). Even worse, it means that those who wear English trousers might be convinced by our reasons for thinking that the Indian apron is superior and decide to start wearing it. The Indian apron, in other words, would cease to have the power to mark our difference if everyone, even those who are not us, were to wear it. This is why Martí insists that these things are better for Latin Americans only given who they are. A concept of culture uncontaminated by race, however, could never claim that we should do or believe something because it is ours, since only what we actually do and believe would count as part of our culture. To say that we should do something because it is ours will always depend on a notion of authenticity grounded in something other than culture. Indeed, this is what the anthropologist Adam Kuper means when he writes that the question of whether someone's cultural identity is authentic requires the a priori assumption that "identity is fixed by descent."[66]

The claim that Martí's anti-universalism is what subverts his antiracism runs counter to a common wisdom that associates race and racialism with universalism. Étienne Balibar's account of neo-racism, for example, explores how *"culture can also function like a nature,* and it can in particular function as a way of locking individuals and groups a priori into a genealogy, into a determination that is immutable."[67] According to Balibar, it is universalism and "the theme of hierarchy" that lurk beneath the surface of neo-racist concepts of culture.[68] However, in the case of Martí, it is the repudiation of the universal and the hierarchical that logically results in a return to biological race. Without hierarchies, culture could never be normative without an appeal to race.

To be precise, it is not that cultural imperatives cannot function without race; it is rather that anti-universalist cultural imperatives cannot function without race. In other words, we can argue that a culture, or part of a culture, should be practiced without recourse to race. However, we cannot argue that only certain people should practice a culture, or part of a culture, without at least an implicit recourse to race. For we would have to explain why certain cultural practices belong only to certain people independent of their actual beliefs and practices. The claim that we should wear an Indian apron because it is part of our identity thus requires us to define our identity before we can decide which cultural practices are better for us. We could not claim that it is the Indian apron that makes us Indian, because if that were the case, we would *already* wear it, and there would be no need for any imperatives that it be worn by us. Likewise, we could not claim that we should wear the Indian apron because it is a tradition that we wear it, since to say it is a tradition implies we are still wearing it, and to realize we no longer wear it is to realize it is no longer a tradition. Cultural imperatives, if they are to be purely cultural, must therefore be universal. Raceless cultural imperatives will always be hostile to difference, but that hostility will never count as a problem because the difference to which they are hostile consists of the cultural practices we have implicitly or explicitly rejected for ourselves. Indeed, to think that our practices are better than others makes nonsense of the value placed on difference: if we decide to wear the Indian apron because we think it is better than the alternatives, we have no reason to want to preserve the difference that it signifies.

It is worthwhile to recall that Martí's repudiation of race, as well as his concept of culture, emerged in the context of larger nationalist, regionalist, and *independentista* projects. Martí was neither the first nor the last Latin American intellectual to prescribe a series of cultural practices in an attempt to affirm or preserve national and regional cultural difference. It is also worthwhile to recognize that "Nuestra América" and the various concepts and arguments that it advances were intended in part as a weapon against global modernity. Such a weapon is as necessary now, at the beginning of the twenty-first century, as it was at the end of the nineteenth. But that should in no way let "Nuestra América" off the hook. Just the opposite—Martí's failure to move beyond an identitarian politics of race reveals the extent to which his project is implicated in the colonial and imperial discourses he wanted to repudiate. The recognition of that fact should at least cast doubt on the efficacy of contemporary formulations that imagine new futures or forms of resistance based on assumptions and claims similar to Martí's. Consider, for example, Aníbal Quijano's influential essay "Modernity, Identity, and Utopia in Latin America" (1993), in which he argues, nearly quoting Martí, that one of the essential, recurring problems in Latin America is the fact that "we read European books and live in a completely different world."[69]

If Martí's antiracist and cultural projects are, as Julio Ramos argues, a "form of resistance to modernization" and a "defense against imperialism," Martí's complicity with racialist discourses of identity signals the limits of that resistance and that defense, especially if we believe that race is part and parcel of colonialism and imperialism.[70] Instead of creating possibilities for autonomy, Martí merely generates a new normativity grounded in race. "Nuestra América" resembles what Kwame Anthony Appiah rightly calls a "politics of compulsion" and is the replacement of "one kind of tyranny with another."[71]

CHAPTER TWO

Beliefs

THE FIGURE IN JOSÉ ENRIQUE RODÓ'S *ARIEL* (1900) that gives the essay its title—Ariel from William Shakespeare's *The Tempest*—is described as an "airy spirit," an immaterial, ascending figure that points to the future triumph of "reason" over "the base impulses of irrationality."[1] Ariel, Rodó suggests, is "the noble, soaring aspect of the human spirit," a figure on the winning side of a historical struggle against Caliban, who is described as the "symbol of brutal sensuality" (31). It could thus be said that Rodó's text is predicated on an ideological disagreement. Whereas Ariel stands for "rational life" (47), "selfless meditation," "ideal contemplation" (87), the "selfless love for beauty" (55), and the "selfless thirst for truth" (82), Caliban stands for the "mode of North American utilitarianism" (48), mediocrity, the "ignorance of all that is subtle and exquisite" (81), the negation of art, "the disintegration of idealism," and the subordination of truth and beauty to "material gain" (85). The difference between Ariel and Caliban, Rodó suggests, is reducible to the difference between true beliefs and values and false ones.

As much as *Ariel* is about beliefs and values, it is also about identity, or what Leopoldo Zea called the affirmation of "the distinct spirit of Latin American peoples."[2] Indeed, the enormous popularity of *Ariel* in the early twentieth century depended not only on its assertion of Ariel's superiority over Caliban but also on its assertion that Ariel represented the essence of Latin American identity. Written during an era when supposedly scientific discourses tended to portray Latin America as racially inferior, socially diseased, or materially backward, *Ariel* located the region's essence in something disembodied and immaterial: the superior beliefs and values derived from a classical European tra-

30

dition that made for "civilized and cultivated individuals" (44). Rodó argued that because the United States sought to "obscure the intellectual superiority and glory of Europe" (86) and replace it with utilitarianism "as the summa and model of civilization" (87), Latin America had "a sacred place in the pages of history that depends upon us for its continuation" (73).

The claim that our essence consists of superior beliefs and values should make us want to celebrate that essence; however, it should not make us want to celebrate the *distinctiveness* of that essence. In fact, just the opposite: to think that what makes Latin America distinctive is its superiority is to be uninterested in preserving its distinctiveness. This is the fundamental contradiction in *Ariel*. On the one hand, *Ariel* calls for the defense of what it casts as "superior" beliefs and values (67); on the other hand, it calls for the protection of the "uniqueness" (73) of "our culture" as defined by the superior beliefs and values it contains (42). If we think that our beliefs and values are superior to the beliefs and values of others, then it makes sense to defend them, but it does not make sense to want them to signify our difference, which would involve wanting inferior beliefs and values to persist just for the sake of our difference. Once we decide, in other words, that Latin American difference consists of superior beliefs and values, we have already abandoned the idea that difference is something to be preserved or celebrated. Rodó thus faces a choice between two positions: either we defend our beliefs and values because they are superior and leave behind our desire that they remain distinctively ours, or we defend our beliefs and values because they are distinctively ours and leave behind the idea that they are superior.[3]

This theoretical problem neither begins nor ends with Rodó. In fact, we can find it in a book that could be called *Ariel*'s polar opposite: Rodolfo Kusch's *Indigenous and Popular Thinking in América* (1970). Besides the fact that they were published seventy years apart, Kusch's text and Rodó's could not appear to be more different: Kusch promotes beliefs grounded in popular indigenous thinking, whereas Rodó champions beliefs derived from elite European discourses. Both Kusch and Rodó, however, confront the intrinsic universality of beliefs, and they both ultimately face a choice between ideology and identity.[4] They choose identity, but they do so at the expense of the contestatory potential of the beliefs they seek to defend and advance.

Kusch's project involves the recovery of an "indigenous view of the world," which he hopes will be able to oppose "the Western attitude."[5] Kusch begins with a discussion of Guaman Poma's "*Mapamundi* of the

Kingdom of the Indies" (1615), which, he complains, has been displaced by so-called scientific maps (4). But Kusch argues for the recovery of the *mapamundi* not because it gives us a truthful picture of the world but rather because it reflects the identity of the person who made it. "What Guaman Poma drew," he writes, "does not accord with reality, but it does encapsulate all of its Indian and Inca inheritance; and whether one likes it or not, it is *his* map" (3). The problem with this claim is that in spite of what might be said about Guaman Poma's map today, Guaman Poma did not merely think of it as *his* map—he thought of it as *the* map, the one that represented "reality." Kusch, however, repudiates the idea of a true map. If no map can claim to be a true map, then what matters about a map is the extent to which it reveals the perspective of its maker. Kusch can thus protect difference from the disagreement implied by thinking that a map is true, since if it is true, then it is true for everyone. If no map is true, then there is no reason to reject Guaman Poma's *mapamundi*, but there is also no reason to recover it. Furthermore, if no map is true, then there is no ground from which to critique *anyone's* map, since, as Kusch puts it, "whether one likes it or not," every map will always turn out to be someone's map.

Kusch's arguments have anticipated, and even informed, what Walter Mignolo and others have called "epistemic difference," which is to say, the idea that universal truths are impossible because different local standards are used to decide what is true. Indeed, Eduardo Mendieta is right to point out that "one of the accomplishments of the decolonial turn" has been the revelation that "epistemic universality, universality as such, is an elusive, nay impossible standpoint."[6] However, the fact that people have different epistemic systems is why they disagree, and it is only because they are committed to the universal validity of their epistemic systems that they can disagree in the first place. But the problem with the critique of epistemic universalism is not only philosophical but also political. Indeed, the concept of "epistemic difference" blunts the oppositional force of our beliefs and eliminates the possibility that our beliefs might be false by abandoning the chance that they might be true. In the end, we are left with the idea that the only justification for our beliefs is that they are ours.

It would be hard to overstate the impact of *Ariel* at the turn of the twentieth century. The publication of *Ariel* almost instantly had far-reaching political and cultural repercussions throughout the region. Pedro Henríquez Ureña captured the importance of *Ariel* when he wrote that "from Mexico and the Antilles to Argentina and Chile, everyone was reading and talking about *Ariel*."[7] Even though the zenith of *arielismo* was between 1905 and 1915, it left an indelible mark on an entire generation of Latin American intellectuals that included Alfonso Reyes and Pedro Henríquez Ureña.[8] As Nicola Miller suggests, *arielismo* "played an acknowledged part in Vasconcelos's theory of the cosmic race; in Argentine Manuel Ugarte's development of a political (rather than cultural) anti-imperialism; in the University Reform Movement of 1918 and in the subsequent political radicalization of the student community that led to the foundation of the American Popular Revolutionary Alliance (APRA) and the Cuban Communist Party."[9] Nevertheless, *arielismo* had nearly as many critics as admirers, ranging from Francisco García Calderón, who claimed in *La creación de un continente* (1913) that *Ariel* was "premature in nations where the capital, which is a tiny nucleus of civilization, is surrounded by a vast semi-barbarous zone," to Jorge Abelardo Ramos, who complained in his *Historia de la nación latinoamericana* (1968) that Rodó proposed "a return to Greece, but failed to explain how the Indians, mestizos, and peons of Latin America might meditate in their farms or cane fields on a superior culture."[10] There was also, of course, "Caliban: Notes Toward a Discussion of Culture in Our America" (1971), in which Roberto Fernández Retamar famously declared that "our symbol [. . .] is not Ariel, as Rodó thought, but rather Caliban."[11] *Ariel* also instigated a series of polemics about culture and politics that continue in the present, and we need look no further than John Beverley's recent characterization of anti-subalternist arguments as "neo-Arielism" to see the extent to which this is the case.[12]

Ariel participated in a cultural and political sea change in the wake of both the defeat of Spain in the Spanish-Cuban-American War (1898) and the clear emergence of U.S. imperialism.[13] In the years immediately following 1898, U.S. military and economic influence throughout the region grew rapidly: the United States established a military base in Cuba, took control of the Panama Canal Zone, and dramatically increased its economic investment throughout the region (between 1897 and 1908, for example, U.S. investment in Mexico grew from $200 million to $672 million).[14] Not surprisingly, the year 1898 also marked the beginning of an extremely adversarial period (1898–1933) in the history of Latin America–U.S. relations.[15]

The hostility toward the United States that characterized this period can be seen in Rubén Darío's "El triunfo de Calibán" (1898). Two years before the publication of *Ariel*, Darío invoked Ariel and Caliban from *The Tempest* to represent the difference between the United States and Latin America.[16] In fact, Darío described Latin America's predicament as the fulfillment of José Martí's worst fears: "Martí never ceased to warn the nations that shared his blood to be careful with those vultures."[17] Darío then asked, "What would that Cuban say today upon seeing that, under the pretext of giving aid to the desired Pearl of the Caribbean, the monster has swallowed it with the oyster and all?"[18]

Ariel also appeared at a time when positivist discourses tended to represent Latin America as a sick body.[19] Texts such as Francisco Bulnes's *El porvenir de las naciones hispano americanas* (1899), César Zumeta's *Continente enfermo* (1899), Agustín Álvarez's *Manual de patología política* (1899), Carlos Octavio Bunge's *Nuestra América* (1903), and Manuel Ugarte's *Enfermedades sociales* (1905) led to a pessimism among Latin American intellectuals regarding the future of the region.[20] These texts attributed Latin America's supposed backwardness to factors such as climate, racial inferiority, nutrition, and racial "instincts." Moreover, as Alejandro Mejías-López has argued, by the end of the nineteenth century, modernization had become associated not with a monolithic sense of "modern Europe" and the United States but with the Anglo-Saxon race, so that a specifically "British and Anglo American modernization became *the* measure of modernization."[21]

Unlike the dominant discourses of the period that disparaged Latin America as inferior, *Ariel* celebrated the superiority of Latin America's essence and called for its preservation. *Ariel* all at once named Latin America as the heir to a great Western European tradition, offered a programmatic critique of the United States, repudiated economic prosperity and technological achievement as markers of progress, and celebrated Latinity over Anglo-Saxon utilitarianism. Furthermore, *Ariel* defined Latin America's essence in terms of disembodied beliefs and values—rather than in terms of embodied instincts—and predicted Latin America's victory over the fleeting "material triumphs" of the United States (79). Indeed, these radical propositions crystallized a wide range of political, cultural, and economic concerns into a seemingly coherent ideology. However, the tensions and contradictions at the heart of *Ariel* are visible in its first pages, where Rodó posits *two* competing Ariels: one is an immaterial ideal, and the other is the material Ariel "preserved" in bronze (32). In these two Ariels, we can already see an anxiety about the immateriality that Rodó's text is perhaps best known for celebrating. In fact, the two Ariels correlate with the essay's two competing and contradictory drives: on the one hand, the exaltation of ideals and "superior qualities" (67), and on the other hand, the desire to protect the "uniqueness" of our culture (72).

Ariel—who represents "the ideal"—is described in terms of a certain uncontrollability: he is "fanciful" and "soaring"; he possesses an "ideal airiness" and is capable of vanishing "in a flash of light" (31–32). Even though Ariel "dominated the room," he does so only in the form of "an exquisite bronze" that captures him on the verge of being set free, in the "instant he is about to take wing and vanish" (31). It is as if, were it not for the bronze, Ariel might not even be in the large classroom, for he would have taken flight and disappeared.[22] The bronze blunts Ariel's force and neutralizes Ariel's exalted qualities: his immateriality, boundlessness, lack of fixity, and violent forcefulness. The once "fanciful figure" (31) becomes a weighty bronze, a "solid sculpture" that is the product of a fundamentally conservative desire to "preserve" Ariel's "beginnings of flight" (32).[23] The bronze Ariel, then, has a contradictory existence: it is motion frozen, a projection into the future stopped in time, a violent force made serene, and an airy spirit made material.

One of the most vexing contradictions in *Ariel* is between *Ariel*'s materialism and its idealism.[24] *Ariel* has often been viewed as a text that replaces material and racial determinism derived from positivism with an idealism in which changeable, ethereal beliefs and ideals are the forces that explain social reality. Some critics, however, such as Charles A. Hale, have questioned the extent to which *Ariel* can be viewed as an idealistic rejection of positivist ideologies.[25] In fact, Jaime Concha perspicaciously argues that the "cardinal paradox" of *Ariel* is that such a "spiritualistic text" appears to be undergirded by a Newtonian conception of physics.[26] *Ariel*, he argues, which "in the name of idealism seeks to condemn moral materialism (the dominant utilitarianism of the North), constantly returns to the terminology of scientific materialism for support."[27]

Maarten Van Delden, however, finds elements of both orientations in *Ariel*, and he argues that they coexist "in an arbitrary, unsystematic manner."[28] For Van Delden, the reasons for the contradictory and "unsystematic" coexistence of positivism (which stresses essentially physical and material explanations of reality) and idealism (which emphasizes the primacy of ideas and beliefs) are strategic and rhetorical: Rodó uses terms and anecdotes "drawn from the researches of natural scientists" because they promise to be "effective in the pursuit of a socio-political goal."[29] Van Delden sees Rodó as primarily interested in affirming idealism. That idealism, he suggests, gets inadvertently compromised given the rhetoric that Rodó instrumentally deploys. However, in the thought of Alfred Fouillée—a prominent idealist critic of materialism in nineteenth-century France and a crucial source for Rodó's own ideas—we can also find materialism and idealism in a tense coexistence.[30] Understanding why that is the case allows us to reconsider the relationship between materialism and idealism in *Ariel*.

Fouillée is widely recognized as the most important source for *Ariel*—Charles A. Hale, for example, calls him Rodó's "principal intellectual guide."[31] In particular, Fouillée's concept of "force-ideas" informed Rodó's model for the diffusion of superior values in Latin America.[32] Fouillée believed that the competition of ideas is what drives societal progress and change. Fouillée, however, recognized the threat to national distinctiveness implied in his model, which is to say, he understood that the very ideas and beliefs that explained change also threatened difference. As a result, he attempted to find ways to protect national distinctiveness from the implications of his own theories, which threatened it. Fouillée, for example, believed that the essence of France could be found in the commitment of its citizens to universal ideas. The problem is that if the essence of being French is having universal beliefs, then the desire to preserve French difference ceases to make much sense, since in this model, the difference between France and the rest of the world is the difference between true beliefs and false ones. Even though Fouillée seems to doubt the relevance of racial factors, he ultimately returns to them to stave off the threat to French distinctiveness implied by beliefs and ideas.[33]

"Indeed it is irrational," writes Fouillée, "to love liberty for one's own sake."[34] Fouillée thus affirms the superiority of what he calls "a general outlook" in which one is concerned with "general and disinterested ideas" (18). For Fouillée, "disinterested" implies "looking toward the *universal*," which is superior because "an *idea*, a pure idea, can begin to confer something of its worth upon us from the very moment of its conception, and if the value of this idea is not particular, if the idea contains a conception of the universal, the value of the will which it guides or directs will itself come to be of an altogether different kind from egoistic interests or egoistic forces" (182). Fouillée believes that evolution and progress are achieved by the desire to convert ideas into actions, to make the ideal real. Even though he argues that "to think of anything, indeed, is already to set about it," he also argues that "there are among ideas some which are superior to all others, which express ideals," and these are what he calls "force-ideas," the "intellectual motor agencies" that drive human progress (179–180). Because force-ideas link "idea and desire" and are characterized by a "disinterestedness looking toward the *universal*," they have implications for "me, as well as you" (182).[35]

But for Fouillée, such ideas also constitute the essence of France: "our national spirit" (22), he writes, is defined by a commitment to "general and universal ideas" (16). He argues that France "is the only country that makes war for the sake of an idea," adding that in France, unlike in England and Germany, where preoccupations focused on the local and the material, ordinary people are "guided by writers" to strive "in the cause of intellectual interests, of philosophical ideas" (20–21). What makes France unique is that it perceives "from the point of view of the philosopher" that "the rights of the Frenchman cannot exist without the rights of man in general" (18). "We ought to love liberty," Fouillée writes, "for the sake of others, as well as for its own sake" because "it is thus that it acquires, like reason, a universal bearing; it is thus that it becomes equality" (18). The trouble is that France's "national spirit," inasmuch as it consists of "the very *universality* of our desires," is "somewhat contagious" and spreads "rapidly from nation to nation" (22). If France is distinctive because of its commitment to "the universal idea over particular facts," then France's distinctiveness consists of the paradoxical desire to bring an end to its own distinctiveness (30). What is "*rational*" and "*universal*," writes Fouillée, "has naturally an expansive, sympathetic power by which other wills are swept along," and "in desiring for others, we have often led others to desire as we do" (22).

Thus the very Frenchness that is defined by the supposed universality of France's beliefs threatens to undo itself as a "national trait" (14). Fouillée declares that he "had no liking for the clean-cut and systematic classifications in which the advocates of the race theory take such satisfaction" (1). But if the national character of France is to be found in its "love of anything which is general and applicable to all humanity," it is easy to see how this is a weak foundation for a national character (17). Indeed, Fouillée writes that the fulfillment of that "love" is "the accord of every mind with all other minds, of every nation with all other nations" (23). Notions such as "the rights of man," which he sees as a mark of the "preoccupation with justice" that is "a tradition of France" (14), lead naturally, he notes, to a "social proselytism" (24).

Even if ideals such as "the rights of man" have their origins in France, it would be hard to see why one would want to view them as distinctively French, given that the force of an idea such as "the rights of man" lies in its universality. It would also be hard to see how "the rights of man" could function as the basis of a national identity, since to believe in them is to believe not only that everyone has them but also that everyone should believe in them as well. Fouillée's solution involves ontologizing beliefs and linking them to material factors such as race and climate. By anchoring France's spirit, which is not "national and exclusive," to the "geographical situation of France" and the "native faculties of our race," Fouillée is thus able to secure France's universality as its distinctive trait.

"The main seat of the imitative part of our nature is our belief," declares Rodó in a key chapter of *Ariel* on the United States, quoting from Walter Bagehot's *Physics and Politics* (1873). What is striking is that the reference to Bagehot's claims about imitation and belief appears in the heart of *Ariel*'s longest and best-known chapter, which deals with the potential dangers of Latin America's "USA-*mania*" (21) and the resultant attempts to impose "a foreign model" onto the region at the expense of its "irreplaceable uniqueness" (72).

In *Ariel*'s chapter on the United States, imitation is cast in negative terms, and Rodó's reference to Bagehot makes it seem as if Bagehot were casting both imitation and belief in a negative light. However, for Bagehot, imitation, or what he calls "the innate tendency of the human mind to become like what is around it," is what explains human progress.[36] In *Ariel*, for the most part, Rodó would agree.

In the same chapter, however, Rodó argues that the belief in the superiority of North American political, cultural, and spiritual ideals constituted a threat to Latin American distinctiveness. This belief is threatening not only because "conviction" is a "passive" mode of imitation but also because, as Rodó writes, "from admiring to imitating is an easy step" (71). Beliefs about North American superiority thus pointed directly to a haunting "vision of an America de-Latinized of its own will, without threat of conquest, and reconstituted in the image and likeness of the North" (71). Rodó's initial response to this threat is an affirmation of Latin American superiority that elides the region with the figure of Ariel. Even though the figure of Ariel is celebrated for being relentlessly aspirational and seeking to rise above the "clinging vestiges" of Caliban, Rodó denounces the "eager mimicry of the prominent and the powerful" as a "kind of political snobbery," and he condemns the desire to "ape the caprices and foibles of those at the peak of society" (72). It is almost possible to say that *Ariel* contains two incompatible texts: one asserts the primacy of ideas and beliefs, whereas the other (consisting primarily of the chapter on the United States) asserts the primacy of identity against the threat to identitarian difference posed by the nature of ideas and beliefs.

The incompatibility of these assertions extends far beyond *Ariel*. We may recognize that all ideals, including the ones we espouse, originate in specific historical moments and cultural contexts, but to espouse an ideal is to dismiss such origins as irrelevant. This is what James Rachels means when he writes that "facts about the differences between cultural outlooks" are irrelevant to the status of the moral ideals that emerge from each cultural outlook; the fact that "different cultures have different moral codes" should not lead us to conclude that "there is no objective 'truth' in morality," and the fact that "opinions vary from culture to culture" should not lead us to conclude that "right and wrong" are mere "matters of opinion."[37] Rachels argues that such conclusions are fundamentally unsound because "the conclusion does not really follow from the premise": the premise "concerns what people *believe*," while the conclusion "concerns *what really is the case*" (153). Against those who would argue that the commitment to transcultural standards is a form of racism, Rachels claims that the critique of racism is impossible without the commitment to transcultural standards. To illustrate this point, he considers a "violently anti-Semitic" society whose leaders have "set out to destroy the Jews"; for Rachels, saying "that a society tolerant of Jews is *better* than the anti-Semitic society" inevitably depends on a "transcultural standard of comparison" (154). Ideals, in other words, are inevitably transcultural even though they emerge from cultural particulars; the fact that ideals are the product of cultural and historical particulars has no bearing on the question of whether or not ideals are true. In fact, if we believe that no ideals are anchored in the universal, the fact that our own ideals are not anchored there can hardly count as a strike against them. Nowhere is this more visible than in the anti-universalist argument against transcultural ideals, which must put forward in circular fashion a transcultural ideal *against* transcultural ideals (not all cultures, after all, respect other cultures).

In *Ariel*, of course, the commitment to the superiority of certain beliefs over others is essential to what Rodó calls "spiritual selection," which relies on "a sense for order and hierarchy and an almost religious aspect for genius" (70). This is the engine that drives the project of *Ariel*, because Ariel, who symbolizes the "noble, soaring aspect of the human spirit" and "the superiority of reason and feeling over the base impulses of irrationality," is in fact "the ideal" that will destroy "the clinging vestiges of Caliban," the "symbol of brutal sensuality" (31). Indeed, Rodó's commitment to hierarchies is demonstrated by the dominance of vertical spatial associations and movements in *Ariel*. "Ariel's irresistible strength," he writes, "is fueled by the ascendant movement of life" (98); Ariel's light shines "above souls that have surpassed the natural limits of humankind" (98); the "impulses" of all "organic life" are "ascendant" (69). Rodó affirms "higher morality" (49) and "higher principles" (55); he celebrates those who "rise above the multitudes"

(33); he is suspicious of moral criteria that are made to "sink" (83); and he condemns egalitarianism because it "bring[s] everyone down" (68). This vertical spatiality accords with the hierarchical terms that abound in *Ariel*: the "superior mode of life" (47); the "superior qualities" such as "virtue, character, and mind" (67); the responsibility of the "superior mind" (68); and the importance of "superior example" (69).

Moreover, Rodó initially affirms that the imitative nature of beliefs is what will bring about the desired order. The youth he speaks to will be of "those groups and peoples who rise above the multitudes" to actually transform others (33). Rodó then refers to Ariel's "conquest of souls" through the strength and will of the youth who will "transmit" their "work" to others (100). In fact, Rodó emphasizes that "the gifts derived from refined taste, the mastery of gracious modes, the delicacy of altruism are [. . .] identified with the 'genius of propaganda,'" by which he means, "the all-powerful gift of universality" (54–55).

Echoing Fouillée, Rodó declares that "to possess these qualities is to possess the *humanity* the French impart to the things they choose to consecrate" (55), by which he means that believing in something as a true ideal requires thinking of it as universal—otherwise, it could hardly be called an ideal in the first place. Rodó groups together ideals with notions such as "universality," "propaganda," and the will to "impart" because that is in fact what ideals necessarily involve. In Rodó's theory of human progress, this is the mechanism by which the world improves: whether or not ideas are "widely disseminated" and long lasting depends on "their greater allure" (55). The way this works is made clear in *Ariel*'s final lines, where Enjolras, the student, declares as he watches "the passing throng" that people "are not gazing at the sky" but "the sky is gazing at them" (101). "Something," he says, is "descending from above upon these indifferent masses," a group that he describes as fertile, "newly turned earth" (101). "The scintillation of the stars is like the movement of the sower's hands," he says, thereby revealing the dynamic that Rodó sees at work: the downward flowing of the light of the stars will produce the new growth that moves upward from the darkness of the soil toward the light of the stars (101).

Rodó's hope for the future is that students who have listened to Prospero's speech will go out into the world and convince others of the superiority of their beliefs and values through arguments. Prospero, after all, teaches his students how to argue and to convince others: if, he says, "a man is to be convinced *not to drive the swallows from his house,* then you must not argue the bird's monastic grace, nor its legendary virtue, but convince the householder that the nests can remain in place without damaging the roofs on which they are built" (56). The question of how and what Prospero tells the youth to argue is less important than the fact that he tells them to argue in the first place. That is to say, Prospero's imperative depends on at least two presuppositions about beliefs and truth: first, that what we think to be true is true for everyone, even those who do not share our beliefs (hence our desire to argue and convince them); second, that the reasons we invoke to justify our beliefs (our epistemic norms) are not merely the ones we happen to have but actually the right ones (hence our appeal to them in an argument and, we could add, our ability to engage in the argument to begin with).[38] To put this another way, if Prospero were to believe, following Santiago Castro-Gómez, that there is no "single way of knowing the world," or that making the world a better place involves establishing an "epistemical democracy," then his imperative to "convince the householder" to change his views, not to mention his confidence in the mere possibility of persuasion, would make no sense.[39]

Disagreements depend on the universal, and in turn, Platonic and Socratic dialogues depend on opposition and disagreement. Roberto González Echevarría reminds us that *Ariel* has an "obvious [. . .] generic identification" with "the classical dialogue."[40] Indeed, as González Echevarría points out, from the very start of *Ariel*, "it is impossible to deny the dialogic appearance of the essay: the master (Socrates, no doubt, as deduced from the slightly paternalistic tone), surrounded by his disciples-friends in a casual, yet organized session."[41] The crucial assumption in such a dialogue, of course, is that "the truth would presumably emerge from the dialectic established between the various points of view."[42] Prospero asserts that his words are meant to be "persuasive" to "young mind[s]," which are "hospitable soil" for new ideas (32). Moreover, he declares that "the evolution of ideas" is to be achieved by each generation's "intellectual activity" and pursuit of "the ideal" (33). To that end, Prospero urges the discovery of the unknown, celebrating those whose hearts were "inspired by visions of bountiful and remote lands" (33). Indeed, *Ariel*'s opening lines abound with imperatives to go "Onward!," declarations that "art, philosophy, free thought, [and] scientific curiosity" are "God-given stimuli" (35), and references to the "generative force" of "ideas" (36).

In lines that are regularly invoked to indicate *Ariel*'s cosmopolitanism, Rodó declares, "I have always disagreed with those who appointed themselves as watchdogs over the destiny of America and as custodians of its tranquility zealously attempted to stifle, even before it reaches us, any resonance of human sorrow, any echo of foreign literatures" (38).

This is because, Rodó argues, "every problem that doubt can pose to the human intellect, every sincere rebuke hurled from the breast of dejection and sorrow against God or Nature, deserves our serious consideration" (38–39). Rodó condemns the "painful isolation in which we Latin peoples live" and calls for "the need for a revitalization" and the "revelation of new strengths" (40). In other words, Rodó's call to the youth depends on an infinitely open, undefined future possibility that they can and must discover through intellect. But such discoveries will be hostile to established tradition and cultural continuity because, as Prospero declares, they will involve the young teaching the old.

Rodó goes to great lengths to celebrate a marketplace of ideas because he believes that human progress is achieved through what he calls "spiritual selection" or "the exaltation of life" (59). In fact, his examples of human progress function within this logic: the "most precious and fundamental of the acquisitions of the spirit—the alphabet, which lends immortal wings to the word—was born in the very heart of Canaanite trading posts, the discovery of a mercantile civilization that used it for exclusively financial purposes" (89). The Canaanites, Rodó means to say, never dreamed "that the genius of superior races would transfigure it, converting it into a means of communicating mankind's purest and most luminous essence" (89). Rodó declares that Egypt is characterized by a "sterile order" because it was a "civilization that existed only to weave its shroud and build its sepulchers" (35). Of course, for all these reasons, *Ariel* is most regularly associated with cosmopolitanism.

The parable of the Hospitable King is often invoked as a key expression of *Ariel*'s cosmopolitanism.[43] In the parable, which González Echevarría calls one of the "rhetorical centers of the essay," a patriarchal King "who lived in the fabled and uncomplicated Oriental lands" lives in a castle that is radically "open" (45).[44] "Freedom and liveliness reigned within this majestic edifice," writes Rodó; "old men gathered" in the castle, "birds flocked at midday to peck crumbs from his table, and [. . .] rolling bands of children ran to the foot of the bed where the silver-bearded King slept" (45). "Deep within, very deep within" the castle, however, "isolated," "hidden," and "secret," the King had a room enclosed by "thick bulwarks," where "not an echo from the boisterous world outside [. . .], not a word from human lips, penetrated the carved porphyry that lined the walls or stirred the air in the forbidden retreat" (46).

Prospero interprets the fable in this way: "your inner life is like this parable," he says, and it "contains a hidden and mysterious cell where no profane guest, only serene reason, may enter" (47). Obviously, the parable accords with *Ariel*'s interest in classical *otium* and links it to the *modernista* "*reino interior*," which Gerard Aching rightly identifies as "the movement's most frequently identified trope."[45] It is curious that a text so committed to cosmopolitanism—or an end to the "painful isolation in which we Latin peoples live"—is also committed to isolation as the key to "freedom" (47). This is further complicated when it becomes clear that all the attributes ascribed to the King's private sanctuary are the *opposite* of those ascribed to Prospero's classroom. The classroom is illuminated by a "beam of light" (32); in the sanctuary, light is "filtered through stained glass" (46). The material surroundings in the classroom are "austere" (31); in the sanctuary, they are ornate. Dialogue supposedly occurs in the classroom; in the sanctuary, there is silence. Moreover, the upward and outward motions in *Ariel* are reversed in the King's sanctuary, which is described as "very deep" (46). In the final part of the parable, it is noted that the King's "thoughts were polished like pebbles by the tide" (47), thus replacing the chiseling that was featured prominently at the beginning of the text with a more gradual—and nature-driven—metaphor for change.

Rodó's idealism reaches its limits in these passages, in the very recognition of the universality of beliefs and their threat to notions of difference. To think that our values are superior, and our beliefs are true, is a weak and troubled ground for retaining regional distinctiveness. As a result, Rodó's text exchanges the superiority of our beliefs for our identity with them. In the section of *Ariel* on the United States, Rodó declares that "we have a heritage of race, a great ethnic tradition" to "maintain" (73). At the beginning of the text, Prospero told his students to espouse beliefs because they were superior; now such beliefs are to be espoused because they are part of our "heritage of race."

Arleen Salles has recently studied the issue of race in *Ariel*, and she questions the extent to which Rodó understands race in purely "sociocultural terms," as many critics have suggested.[46] Indeed, Rodó's commitment to theories of imitation combined with his fear that Latin Americans might imitate the United States to the point of being "de-Latinized" suggests a view incompatible with a classical, deterministic account of race. On the other hand, when Rodó claims that "nature has not gifted [North Americans] with a genius of persuasion or with the vocation of the apostle," he seems to view race as an unchanging and inescapable essence that undeniably determines who people are (87). Ultimately, however, the point is not that Rodó's "use of the term [race] is not always clear and coherent" but rather that the discourse of race, which reaches a crescendo in *Ariel*'s chapter on the United States—with its anxious references to "denaturalizing" national characters (72), a "de-Latinized" Latin America (71), the need to "protect the uniqueness of our personal character," "fidelity" to "the past" (73), and the dangers of "artificial" imitation (72)—functions as an identitarian correction to its idealism.[47] A text that begins with radical change projected into the future becomes obsessed with *maintaining, preserving,* and *continuing.*

A strikingly similar tension between identity and beliefs emerges in Kusch's *Indigenous and Popular Thinking in América*, a text that many readers might view as a radical repudiation of everything for which Rodó's text stands. But both texts confront a recurring problem in Latin American thought. If to believe something is to believe that it is true, then it is hard to see how beliefs can ever be truly *ours.* In other words, if we believe that something is true, then we believe that it is true for everyone, even those who do not believe it. Inasmuch as we think that people should have true beliefs and not false ones, we want our beliefs to be shared by others, which is to say, to be more than merely *ours.*

Kusch writes that Guaman Poma's "*Mapamundi* of the Kingdom of the Indies" (1615) allowed him to see with "clarity the radical contrast that runs through everything American" (2). As Kusch points out, Guaman Poma's map is "oval shaped, and in its center one finds four couples ruling the four cardinal points, with a sun and a moon presiding over the picture and a series of monsters disseminated throughout its contours" (2–3). As such, Kusch notes, Guaman Poma's map is "incommensurate with a modern map of Perú," one that is thought to be "scientifically in sync with reality" because it is "made with modern instruments" (3). Guaman Poma's map and a modern map of Peru, in other words, seem to be in conflict with each other, since each of them represents the mapmaker's belief about the truth of *what is.* The modern mapmaker relies on science, whereas Guaman Poma was relying on what Walter Mignolo refers to in *The Darker Side of the Renaissance: Literacy, Territoriality, and Colonization* (1995) as "a cognitive structure that could be interpreted as a transformed memory of the Inca Tahuantin-suyu, a native cognitive structure, corresponding with the view of the universe in Andean cosmology."[48] Both maps, nevertheless, represent the world as each mapmaker sees it and believes it to exist. Although each mapmaker might work from within a different cognitive structure, they both, nevertheless, believe that their maps are true. Kusch, however, laments the fact that Guaman Poma's map is today "discarded" (3), despite that fact that it is not the map "statistically accepted by the majority" (4).

Kusch argues that "between us and Guaman Poma lies a different conception of the world," which is obvious given the difference in the maps (113). Kusch, however, wants to find a way for the two maps to be somehow reconciled with each other, so that the maps would be understood in terms outside of questions of truth or falsity. Kusch wants the two maps to be understood as merely different, and of equal value—instead of judging the maps in terms of their reflection of "reality," Kusch prefers that the maps be seen as reflections of the subjectivity that produced them. In this way, each map would merely reflect its maker's own particular way of thinking and his subjective vision of what is. Thus, Kusch suggests, "the difference between Guaman Poma and a Spanish chronicler such as Montesinos," for example, "can be seen in two ways" (114). "Either Guaman Poma is inferior to Montesinos," he writes, "or each utilizes a distinct style of thinking" (114). Kusch's point is not that Guaman Poma's map is actually the one that *truly* "accord[s] with reality" but rather that there are merely different particular realities, none with a singular claim to be *the* reality.

It is as if for Kusch the very existence of multiple maps reveals the impossibility of universal truths: since each person judges the validity of someone else's map from within his or her "distinct style of thinking," Kusch suggests that there are no impartial grounds from which to decide which map is true. As Kusch's reasoning goes, if people were to claim the truth of one map over another, they would only do so from *within* their "distinct style of thinking" and their distinct, local, historically and culturally situated rationality. Thus for Kusch, everyone's map must always be true, since each map reflects the point of view from which it was made. Because there are no neutral, universal grounds from which to adjudicate disagreements between two ways of seeing the world, Kusch concludes that there must be no such thing as universal truth.

In this light, Guaman Poma's map is neither true nor false but merely a reflection of one of many realities—in this case, the "vital world [. . .] of the Indian"—and as such has "little or nothing to do with the *real* world detected by science, but rather with the *reality* lived daily by each person" (5). According to Kusch, "what Guaman Poma drew does not accord with reality, but it does encapsulate all of its Indian and Inca inheritance; and whether one likes it or not, it is *his* map—the real habitat of his community" (3). Thus, "in the final analysis," he writes, "the Perú Guaman Poma traversed must have been the one reflected in his map and not the one plotted by contemporary science" (3). This argument can be understood as a version of what has been called "relativism," or in the words of Ruth Groff, the idea that "all knowledge claims are equally well justified."⁴⁹ Paul Boghossian calls this the doctrine of "equal validity," which is to say, the idea that "there are many radically different, yet 'equally valid' ways of knowing the world, with science being just one of them."⁵⁰

The problem as Kusch sees it is not only that Guaman Poma's map is discarded because it is "subjective," but also that some maps are embraced because they are "objective" (16). He argues that an objective map, or a map created "from the *scientific* angle," is "an impersonal map" that can be made "while living in another country" (4). Kusch's notion of "impersonal" implies universality—the idea that something is true for everyone everywhere whether they believe it or not, a truth that transcends differences in subject position.

The "impersonal map," then, not only would "have nothing to do with what Peruvians think of their country," but also would threaten the very content of "what Peruvians think of their country" by implying that there are "impersonal" truths that could be invoked to repudiate personal ones. As Kusch himself emphasizes, the challenge facing the recovery of indigenous thinking is the existence of "an attitude that is expressed in universal terms evacuated of the entirety of the geographic continent" (154). The "attitude" of "universal terms," he argues, casts Latin America as "black, passive, and retrograde, a fountain from which spring tyrants and undesirable populations" (154). Moreover, he insists, "the middle class knows that [. . .] it would like to recover the ingenuousness of Guaman Poma to initiate the great heroic phase with the *así* of the surrounding world" (149). But before that can be achieved, Kusch declares, "it is necessary for it to lose its fascination" with knowledge—or what he calls "nameables" (150). Therefore, Kusch replaces the universality of any one "particular way of thinking" (103) with a sense of the equal validity of all "conception[s] of the world" (103). If there are merely different, equally valid ways of seeing the world, then the implicit conflict between the two maps disappears.

Guaman Poma's map—and the question of how to understand it—is thus a crucial point of departure for Kusch, because embedded in the very possibility of asserting one map's accuracy, truthfulness, or objectivity over another is the essence of what Kusch wants to dismantle. The idea is that once we realize that claims to truth always emerge from particular—rather than universal—subject positions, then claims about what is true automatically become claims about what is true for us, given who we are. This line of thinking protects our beliefs from the universalism involved in questions of truth and falsity, and it also turns our beliefs into reflections of our identitarian difference. However, this line of thinking means that our identitarian difference is the only fact we can invoke to justify the beliefs we have. In the prologue to the first edition of *Indigenous and Popular Thinking in América*, for example, Kusch declared that "questionnaires, dialectical Marxism, public education, universal suffrage, or spiritual values are the slogans of an active América, but at base they are nothing but the thinking of an enterprising middle class, situated in the coastal cities of the continent" (lxxvi). "That is why," he continued, "when a peasant does not want to know anything about Marxism or development, it is not because of ignorance of underdevelopment" (lxxvi). On the contrary, he argues, it is because "the peasant's personality, just like his cultural world, rotates around a different axis" (lxxvi).

Kusch's vision of disagreement as merely the difference between cultural worlds is made possible by his theorization of the difference between *ser* and *estar*, which he had already begun to develop in an earlier book, *América profunda* (1962).[51] The verb *estar*, Kusch suggests, is not only the key to "recovering [. . .] a style of life" grounded in an "indigenous conception" (164), but also a way of connoting "another sphere of reality," a "non-essential reality," a "world without definitions," and "a world where only circumstance abounds" (160). What appeals to Kusch about the logic of *estar* is its instability, its contingency, and its impermeability by claims about what something is, or what is true, or what is better, that would pretend to transcend particularity and subjectivity. The idea of *estar* for Kusch is about "a decided preference for circumstance" in which there is no "public"—by which he means "universal" or "impersonal"—way to "understand this circumstance" (163). In other words, he suggests, "one is left with a mere *it seems to me*" (164). Kusch needs the concept of *estar* to get around the problems inherent in beliefs, namely, the fact that beliefs are intrinsically and inescapably universalizing. Or to put this in Kusch's own terms, beliefs are, of course, always claims of *it seems to me*, but they also must be, to count as beliefs, claims of *it is*.

It is not, as Immanuel Wallerstein suggests in *Historical Capitalism* (1983), that universalism is a "belief," "faith," "cultural ideal," or even an "epistemology" that can be historically situated.[52] For Wallerstein, "the belief in universalism has been the keystone of the ideological arch of historical capitalism" (81). Moreover, he argues, "universalism is a faith, as well as an epistemology" that "requires not merely respect but reverence for the elusive but allegedly real phenomenon of truth" (81). The origins of this "faith," Wallerstein suggests, are to be found in "the processes involved in the expansion of the capitalist world economy—the peripheralization of economic structures, the creation of weak state structures participating in and constrained by an interstate system" that sought processes of "'westernization,' or even more arrogantly 'modernization'" (82). Thus the expansion of a world economy sought a series of cultural changes, namely, "Christian proselytization; the imposition of European language; instruction in specific technologies and mores; changes in the legal codes" that were "legitimated by the desirability of sharing both the fruits of and faith in the ideology of universalism" (82). The motives for this, Wallerstein argues, were on the one hand "economic efficiency," since if "given persons were expected to perform in given ways in the economic arenas, it was efficient both to teach them the requisite cultural norms and to eradicate competing cultural norms," and on the other hand "political security," since "it was believed that if the so-called elites of peripheral areas were 'westernized,' they would be separated from their 'masses,' and hence less likely to revolt" (82).

This is a familiar position regarding universalism—namely, that it emerged from a particular historical moment of European economic and territorial expansion and can thus be associated with Eurocentrism and an entire legacy of oppression, atrocity, and racism, which Wallerstein explicitly links with universalism. Indeed, according to Étienne Balibar, racism is actually *"one form of* universalism."[53] For Balibar, the link between racism and universalism is not complementary but essential: racism, he argues, is "universal theoretically, meaning that there has to be an element of paradoxical universality in it."[54] The urgent task, Balibar concludes, is to "transform universalism."[55]

But universalism is neither an ideology, nor a faith, nor an epistemology. It is intrinsic to beliefs, and it is thus present in every belief and in every rationality. As Boghossian points out, essential to the possibility of beliefs is their propositional content. A belief, he argues, presupposes "a *truth condition*—how the world would have to be if the belief is to be true" (11). Even though a belief emerges from a particular subject position, the question of its truth or falsity is determined *outside* that subject position—as Boghossian puts it, "my saying it is so doesn't automatically make it so, otherwise there could not be any such thing as a false assertion" (12). Thus beliefs are intrinsically universal, which is another way of saying that something is true or false regardless of whether or not we believe it. Donald Davidson makes the same point when he argues that "it is possible to have a belief only if one knows that beliefs may be true or false."[56] Davidson continues to explain that "I can believe that it is now raining, but this is because I know that whether or not it is raining does not depend on whether I believe it, or everyone believes it, or it is useful to believe it; it is up to nature, not to me or my society or the entire history of the human race."[57] Ultimately, Davidson argues, without "the concept of truth, not only language, but thought itself, is impossible."[58]

Kusch's argument—much like Richard Rorty's on Bellarmine and Galileo—that different beliefs are the product of reasoning from different epistemic systems does not change the fact that the concept of truth makes language and thought possible.[59] In Boghossian's refutation of Rorty, he concedes that disagreements can be reducible to different epistemic systems. The existence of different epistemic systems is often why we have disagreements in the first place. Thus, Boghossian writes, in such a disagreement, "we would have to *justify* the principles of our system over theirs" and "offer them some *argument* that demonstrated the objective superiority of our system over theirs."[60] To do that, however, we would have to use an epistemic system, and "naturally, we would use ours," because the reason it is our epistemic system in the first place is that we take it to be the correct one.[61]

If we believe something, in other words, it is because we think that the reasons for believing it are the right reasons. Otherwise, we would have *different* reasons. As Stanley Fish has argued, it only follows that we will hear someone else's reasons not "*as* reasons, but only as errors or even delusions."[62] Fish explains, for example, that "the central beliefs of Christianity cannot be falsified (or even strongly challenged) by evidence that would not be seen as evidence by those who hold the beliefs."[63] For Fish, "no brute data available and perspicuous apart from our belief provides independent warrant for that belief," and "no event that occurs or word that is spoken (even if spoken by God) bears an inescapable meaning that imprints itself unmistakably on the understanding of all parties."[64] Nevertheless, we must still think that our beliefs are true and that our reasons for believing what we do are the right reasons; to say otherwise makes nonsense of any belief.[65]

Thinking that our beliefs are true, however, means thinking of difference as disagreement. Herein we can begin to see the problem with, as well as the appeal of, Kusch's repudiation of truth. Every community—an indigenous one as much as a scientific one—has reasons for believing what it does, and these are the reasons of the community, but if they are not our reasons, we will conclude that they are the *wrong* reasons. As Susan Haack has suggested, "if one really believed that criteria of justification are purely conventional, wholly without objective grounding, then, though one might conform to the justificatory practices of one's own epistemic community, one would be obliged to adopt an attitude of cynicism towards them, to think of justification always in covert scare quotes."[66] For Haack, the problem is that "one cannot coherently engage fully—non-cynically—in a practice *of justifying beliefs* that one regards as wholly conventional."[67]

Kusch, however, wants to transfer the question of claims and beliefs—about, for example, what things are or what things mean—into the logic of *así*, which is radically outside the questions of "*how* to believe" and "the *what for* and *why* believe" (152). In this way, Kusch's notion of *así* attempts to imagine a way of justifying practices outside of beliefs. Kusch relates an episode in which he visited Chipayas, in the province of Carangas in Bolivia. A witch doctor named Huarachi took his group to "his cylindrical hut, which had a domed roof" (106). One of the members asked the witch doctor why the hut was built the way it was, imagining perhaps that "it must be because it was very windy in that region and a circular house would be warmer in offering less resistance to the wind" (106). The witch doctor never answered, but Kusch, citing the Bolivian archaeologist Carlos Ponce Sanginés, argues that "the circular construction was not related to utility, but rather to tradition: it had irrational roots" (106). The reason for building the huts the way they were built was "custom" (106). Kusch's *así* thus achieves a way of doing things that does not require any beliefs.

This freedom from beliefs is also what is achieved in Kusch's distinction between causal and seminal thinking: in South America, he writes, "there is, on the one hand, an indigenous cultural structure mounted on a thinking through *inward directedness* which personalizes the world," and "on the other hand, there is an urban cultural structure based in a causalist thinking, limited to intellection, volition, the depersonalization of science, and the myth of the solution" (126). Urban bourgeois Latin American culture, Kusch argues, "has been mounted on the exclusion of a seminal thinking" (132), and "science and rationality" are used to repress "seminal thinking" (133). Unlike "the problem of understanding" in the "Western point of view," which commits to "a reality that is given *outside of* us" (10), Kusch's seminal thinking would confine itself "to a negation of all that has been affirmed" (129), and it would be a thinking not of affirmations and claims, of truths and falsities, but instead of "contemplation and waiting, because it withdraws from a commitment to external reality" (130). Moreover, it would give up the questions of "the *how* to believe, the *what for* and *why* believe" in favor of "reassuming a prior attitude, prior to even thinking" and accepting the "*así* of reality" (152). Thus, seminal thinking is both the thinking to which Kusch wants to return and the theory that makes that return available. Seminal thinking, in other words, is the theory that makes way for a so-called return to a culture characterized by seminal thinking itself. As Kusch sees it, only a thinking that rejects absolutism, the universal, and the idea that realities exist *"outside of us"* (10) can make possible "the elaboration of a culture that is our own" (4). In the case of Argentina, Kusch notes, it was an "imported culture" that exerted "pressure [. . .] on our interiority" and hindered "the elaboration of a culture that is our own" (4). Presumably the "pressure" is relieved when the "imported culture" is revealed to be merely one of several ways of knowing and to constitute one of many equally valid belief systems.

Indeed, the notion that all beliefs are equally valid solves one problem—the preservation of difference—but creates another series of problems. If we think of different beliefs as merely different and equally valid ways of seeing the world, then disagreement becomes impossible. Moreover, the desire to convince others to share our way of seeing the world begins to make less sense. The privilege given to a certain epistemic system as something that should be recovered by certain people requires that those beliefs be grounded in something other than the value of the epistemic systems themselves. For if they are equal, we can claim one only because it is ours. But if what is sought is a *change*, we are thus forced to claim that a particular epistemic system is ours even though it is different from the one we currently use.

This is an old question. The polemics surrounding the question of the "originality" or "authenticity" of Latin American philosophy and thought have a long history extending back to Juan Bautista Alberdi's search for an authentically "American philosophy" and continuing through the writings of José Gaos, Leopoldo Zea, Francisco Miró Quesada, and Enrique Dussel, among many others.[68] These debates, however, represent different sides of the same coin: the question of whether or not a set of beliefs is "original" or "ours" (whatever one's position is on that issue) is irrelevant to the question of whether or not that set of beliefs is true. Indeed, the effort to make our identity relevant to the truth of our beliefs is antithetical to the nature of belief.

One noteworthy attempt to circumvent these problems is Augusto Salazar Bondy's *¿Existe una filosofía de Nuestra América?* (1968). In his polemic, Salazar Bondy recognizes the difficulty "negating the veracity of inauthentic philosophies."[69] One could say, he writes, that "these philosophies tell a lie about the being that assumes them, but in telling a lie, they actually tell the truth about the real defect of that person's being," which is another way of saying that our philosophies and beliefs are always authentic inasmuch as we have them (82). Thus, Salazar Bondy has to then affirm that the problem was correcting "the real defect" of Latin American being: "what is certain," he writes, "is that we Latin Americans" have an "inauthentic existence" and "we live within a false self, we have the pretensions of being other than what we truly are" (83). Herein was the crux of the well-known debate between Salazar Bondy and Leopoldo Zea.[70] Salazar Bondy's response to the problem of authentic beliefs sidesteps the problem by locating it in authentic selves, claiming that Latin Americans have to become authentic selves *before* they can have an authentic philosophy. Thus, the change that Salazar Bondy proposes must take place independently of beliefs, and so it must be a turn to something that does not involve beliefs; this actually intensifies the problem that Salazar Bondy set out to solve. For how could a cultural transformation not entail beliefs or philosophical underpinnings? Such a transformation would seem to involve a return to something already within us—not in our minds, but elsewhere. From that self, Salazar Bondy argues, an authentic Latin American philosophy will emerge, but inadvertently, it will be a philosophy linked to an essence that has nothing whatsoever to do with philosophy.

Kusch writes that "the issue" is not to "negate Western philosophy, but to look for a formulation closer to our own lives" (1). His point, of course, is that the problem with Western philosophy is that it is not *ours*. Even though many Latin Americans, Kusch suggests, entertain the fantasy that they "have the freedom to adopt any philosophy," the choice made available to them in *Indigenous and Popular Thinking in América* is ultimately between Western philosophy and "our South Américan truth" (7). In the absence of a negation of Western philosophy, the only justification for "our South Américan truth" can be that it is "our South Américan truth," and we will have to endlessly account for who we are in order to understand why "our South Américan truth" is ours in the first place. However, it could be said that the seemingly paradoxical desire in Kusch's text is for "our South Américan truth" to become ours; the fact that it was *not* ours is what is held up to explain the "deep contradictions that [. . .] tear us apart" (7). This paradoxical position concerning which truths are and are not ours has a number of consequences, not least of which is that we can no longer simply assume that our (supposedly real) truths are identical to what we believe is true. Moreover, our (supposedly real) truths become representative, rather than constitutive, of our identity. Thus, in order to know which truths are really ours, Kusch forces us to appeal to something other than what we happen to think is true in order to account for who we are. The nature of that something is revealed when Walter Mignolo writes, in the introduction to the recent English-language translation of Kusch's book, that "if for any European it would have been difficult to live in the skin of an Indigenous person, there would be reason to assume that an Indigenous person would have difficulty living in the skin of a European."[71] The task, therefore, becomes acquiring and maintaining the philosophy that belongs to your "skin." In the end, however, this does not mean that it is impossible, intrinsically contradictory, or even undesirable to be invested in indigenous thinking as a project. Instead, it means that such a project involves a choice between a commitment to indigenous thinking and a commitment to identity and difference. To choose the latter is to foreclose on the very real possibility that the beliefs and values held by millions of Latin Americans are undergirded by reasons that are not only their reasons but also the right reasons.

CHAPTER THREE

Meaning

ONE OF THE MOST PERVASIVE ORTHODOXIES SUR-
rounding Latin American literature is the explicit or
implicit repudiation of the idea that the meaning of a text is fixed to
what its author intended it to mean.[1] The stakes of that repudiation are
both theoretical and political: in *The Lettered City* (1984), for example,
Ángel Rama associated "semantic fixity" with "official vigilance" and
"forces of repression"; the lettered city, he argued, depended on a "uni-
vocal interpretative system" that "strove to permit one reading only."[2]
However, the logical consequence of repudiating authorial intention
is that interpretative disagreements are converted into descriptions of
the identitarian differences between readers. That is because without
intention, or the idea that a text's meaning exists independently from
our individual experience of it, we cannot have interpretative disagreements. In order to disagree with someone about a text's meaning, we
must think not only that *our* interpretation is in fact *the* interpretation
but also that our different experiences as readers are irrelevant. How
else would it make sense to think that others, who have their own ir-
refutably distinctive experiences of reading a text, can be wrong about
what it means?

In the introduction to her edited volume *The Ethics of Latin American Literary Criticism: Reading Otherwise* (2007), Erin Graff Zivin poses
a provocative question: "Can the act of reading be understood as an
event?"[3] If the answer is "yes," then one consequence is that the identity of the reader must be taken into account, since the reader is actually a participant in the event. Additionally, no two readings or events
of reading will be alike because, among other things, no two readers
will be alike. If reading is thought to be an event, then a full accounting

of the subject position of each reader becomes fundamentally important, since each reading will vary depending on who is doing it, where
it is happening, and when. In fact, the entire range of these variations
will become the focus of our investigations, and we will be left to make
sense of them by describing not the text but rather the endless differences among reading subjects, the place where they are reading, and so
forth.

Graff Zivin alternatively considers what might be gained by exploring other "interrelated avenues of inquiry," such as the role of affect or
the extent to which "we can locate within literary discourse an 'other
side' of representation, some element within the confines of the text (or
within our encounter with the text) that resists representation."[4] However, affect and that which "resists representation" are two sides of the
same coin, since both force us to abandon interpretation in favor of a
description of the subject position of the reader. On the one hand, if
we are interested in a reader's affective response to a text, rather than
interpreting the text we will have to focus on the particularity of the
reader having the affective response. On the other hand, if we are interested in that which resists representation, all we can logically do is
deal with the myriad affective responses it produces, since there is no
representation that we can interpret. Both of these questions, however,
force us to contend with not only the reader's identity but also everything that is part of the reader's experience.

The extent to which this is true is illustrated in Julio Cortázar's classic short story "Continuity of Parks" (1956), in which the reader of a
novel realizes that he is a character in the novel he is reading. It is often
said that "Continuity of Parks" affirms the participation of the reader
in the meaning of a text.[5] However, it could also be said that "Continuity of Parks" points to the consequences involved in thinking of the
reader as a participant, since at the end of Cortázar's story, the reader
discovers not only that he is in the text, but also that everything that
surrounds him (and is thus part of his experience) is in the text as well:
his green velvet armchair, his house, his study, the "great windows,"
and the "oak trees in the park."[6] In fact, it is precisely the repetition of
these elements from the reader's surroundings at the end of the story
that signals his presence in the novel he is reading. Hence the "continuity" of "Continuity of Parks," which is Cortázar's shortest story and, at
least logically, his most endless: if the reader is part of the text, then so
is virtually everything else.

The interest in questions such as the event of reading or the affective response of the reader makes identitarian difference the main fo-

cus of studying a text, but it also destroys the notion of the text as a discrete object that can be studied in the first place. If reading is an event, or if what matters about a text is the affective experiences of its readers, studying literature inescapably involves describing the infinite and irreducible differences among reading subjects over space and time. Just as every reading event will be bound up with an account of the subjective particularity of each reader, so too will the affective responses a text produces. However, whenever readers understand themselves as having read the same text, or whenever readers disagree about what a text means, they have *already* rejected both the idea that reading is an event and the idea that the reader's experiential encounter with the text is relevant to what it means. That is because in order for two people to have an interpretative disagreement, they must first agree that the ontology of the text is fixed and stable. This is not to say that their disagreement will not involve the very question of the text's ontology, only that they will not be able to disagree about the text's meaning or its ontology if they think that its ontology is fluid, unstable, or contingent. Although the two readers need not agree about what the text's ontology is, they must agree that whatever it is, it is fixed and not contingent on its readers (if the text's ontology were bound up with each reader's experience of the text, the two readers would not be disagreeing but rather talking about two different texts, each one made distinct by their participation). Then, having recognized that their individual experience has nothing to do with what the text is, they will have to acknowledge that it makes no sense to justify their beliefs about the text's nature and meaning by referring to themselves or their experience.[7] Instead, both readers will realize that they hold their beliefs about the text because they think those beliefs to be true.

If the nature of interpretation requires us to think that our beliefs about a text's meaning are universally true, this obviously poses a problem for both an intellectual tradition committed to celebrating and preserving identitarian difference and a literary tradition committed to what Pedro Henríquez Ureña called "the search for our genuine expression."[8] As a result, one of the main efforts of Latin American literary criticism has been to find ways out of meaning's universalism, either by replacing arguments about what a text means with descriptions of the effects it produces on readers, or by affirming that meaning is determined not by the author's intention but by the reader's participation.

This, however, is not to say that Latin American literature does not contain exceptions to this tendency. In fact, Jorge Luis Borges's "Pierre Menard, Author of the *Quixote*" (1939) offers one of the best and most lucid theorizations of the nature of literary interpretation.[9] Borges's story, of course, is generally thought to point to the reader's role in the making of meaning. Lisa Block de Behar, for example, sees "Pierre Menard" as "one of the best statements in defense of the reader," and Sylvia Molloy has suggested that it reveals how the "author, narrator, text, and reader shape and are shaped by the text."[10] However, just the opposite is true; Borges's story affirms that meaning has nothing whatsoever to do with either the reader or the context in which a text is read. Moreover, "Pierre Menard" underscores the intrinsic universalism involved in the question of meaning that much Latin American literary criticism and theory has attempted to overcome.

Borges's story is about a French Symbolist poet named Pierre Menard who sets out to write *Don Quixote*.[11] Menard, Borges's narrator tells us, "did not want to compose another *Quixote*—which is easy— but *the Quixote itself*."[12] In other words, Menard did not want merely to copy Cervantes's novel; instead, he wanted to be its author. As Menard explains, "I have taken on the mysterious duty of reconstructing literally [Cervantes's] spontaneous work" (41). In the end, Menard succeeds in producing verbatim versions of "the ninth and thirty-eighth chapters of the first part of *Don Quixote* and a fragment of chapter twenty-two" (39).

In Borges's story, the theoretical questions asked and answered arise from the difference between Menard's *Quixote* and Cervantes's— whether there is a difference at all, and if so, how to define it. The story's narrator compares Cervantes's *Don Quixote* to Menard's identical version and has "a revelation" (43). Despite the fact that the two texts are "verbally identical," the narrator discovers that they are crucially different (42). He notes, for example, that in Menard's text the language "suffers from a certain affectation," whereas in Cervantes's text the author "handles with ease the current Spanish of his time" (43). The narrator then compares two identical passages: "truth, whose mother is history, rival of time, depository of deeds, witness of the past, exemplar and adviser to the present, and the future's counselor" (43).

Borges's narrator dismisses the passage in Cervantes's version as "a mere rhetorical praise of history," but he thinks that, as it appears in Menard's, "the idea is astounding" (43). Given that Menard was "a contemporary of William James," the "final phrases," he declares, "are brazenly pragmatic" (43). The reference to Menard's lines as "pragmatic" is important because it underscores the account of beliefs the story puts forward.[13] The difference between the two texts and their respective meanings in "Pierre Menard" is not grounded in anything objective, but only in a reader's subjective belief about the truth of what each author intended. But rather than conclude that there can then be no true meanings, the narrator concludes the opposite: he writes that "historical truth, for him, is not what happened; it is what we judge to have happened" (43). The point is not that there is no such thing as historical truth but rather that whatever we believe happened in the past is also what we must believe is *the truth about what happened in the past*. Borges's story extends this idea into the realm of interpretation, so that what a text means is what we judge its author to have intended it to mean.

In this way, Borges anticipates Steven Knapp and Walter Benn Michaels's argument in "Against Theory" (1982).[14] In their essay, Knapp and Michaels advance the claim that "what a text means is what its author intends."[15] Indeed, Knapp and Michaels argue that the question of whether or not something is language is the question of whether or not it has an author. To even recognize something as language (and hence meaningful) in the first place, they argue, requires first "positing an author" (728). The question of what exactly language means, then, "will not involve adding a speaker but deciding among a range of possible speakers" (726). Borges's story hinges on the narrator's attribution of a text to different authors or "speakers"—after all, the story's title, "Pierre Menard, Author of the *Quixote*," itself emphatically identifies an author. The title of Borges's story—technically the very first part of it—begins by naming a text and identifying its author, as if to highlight the primacy of authorial intention to the question of meaning.

Borges's narrator notes that it is "astounding" to compare the two texts: when Cervantes writes about "the curious discourse of Don Quixote on arms and letters," the narrator sees sincerity (42). "Cervantes was a former soldier," he notes, so his stance "against letters and in favor of arms" is "understandable" (41). But the same lines in Menard's *Don Quixote* are ironic: Menard, the narrator claims, had the "habit of propagating ideas which were the strict reverse of those he preferred" (42). (It is worth noting that to believe that a text's meaning is what its author intends does not limit interpretation to an author's conscious or explicit intentions, nor to an author's own beliefs about his or her intentions.) The two texts in question in Borges's story are identical, and yet the narrator sees two different texts that mean two different things. This is possible only because the narrator posits two different authors: since the texts are identical, only something external to both the words on the page and the reader's experience could justify thinking that there is a difference between them. This is in part what Borges means when he qualifies a list of Pierre Menard's work that does not include

Don Quixote as merely a list of his "visible work" (37). In the case of Menard's *Don Quixote*, the work is *invisible*: it cannot be seen when the two texts are put side by side, and it is only because the narrator sees the text and then appeals to something that cannot be seen (in other words, Menard's authorship) that Menard's work can then be recognized and evaluated. If meaning were located in the words themselves, there would be no way to distinguish between Cervantes's "mere rhetorical praise of history" and Menard's "brazenly pragmatic" lines (43).

Likewise, if meaning were made by the reader, then the difference between the two texts could never be the kind that Borges's narrator identifies—"archaic" versus "current," for example (43)—which essentially derives from the difference between two authors and their intentions and not the difference between two contexts or experiences of reading. As was the case in Cortázar's "Continuity of Parks," the differences would have to include everything that is part of the reader's experience of the texts, including, for example, the typographical differences between Cervantes's *Don Quixote* and Menard's. A footnote at the end of the story refers to Menard's "peculiar typographical symbols and his insect-like handwriting" (44). Borges's narrator, moreover, emphasizes that "Cervantes's text and Menard's" are only "verbally identical," not visually identical (42). If Borges's point were that the reader's experience mattered to the question of meaning, then his narrator would have had to take into account the visual differences that were undoubtedly part of his experience of the differences between the two texts. We can perhaps assume that Cervantes's *Quixote* was printed, while Menard's was handwritten. But the narrator emphasizes that Menard's real work on his *Quixote* is *invisible*, which means that he has already decided that the visible or material differences between the two texts are irrelevant. The significance of this is easy to overlook, because we do not normally attribute meaning to the particular appearance of an author's handwriting in a manuscript, or even to how the lines are broken in a piece of prose fiction. Likewise, we do not normally assume that two verbally identical but visually different editions of the same text (with different fonts or different line breaks) are in fact two different texts with two different meanings. Indeed, we do not usually attribute meaning to line breaks, fonts, or page numbers because we do not believe that the author intended them to be meaningful. To be sure, they are part of our experience of the text, but they are not usually part of the text itself, and we are able to make that distinction only because we can distinguish between the author's intention and our experience.[16]

The idea that context is relevant to meaning has frequently been affirmed in readings of "Pierre Menard."[17] Beatriz Sarlo, for example, argues that "Pierre Menard" destroys "the idea of the fixed identity of a text" and highlights how "meaning is constructed in a frontier space where reading and interpretation confront the text."[18] For Sarlo, meaning is "not tied to words but to words in a context," which ultimately means that "Borges lays claim to the productivity of reading and demonstrates the impossibility of repetition."[19] But if it were true that repetition is impossible in the act of reading, then no one could ever disagree about a text's meaning because no one would ever be reading the same text. The words might be the same, but the context of the words would be infinitely variable.

How can it make sense to suggest that the difference between the two *Quixotes* in Borges's story is determined by context? Only after we have first posited an author can we go on to establish the historical context; without the appeal to an author, nothing in the text of Menard's *Quixote* can give us the context that would change its meaning. In Borges's story, meaning changes not when texts are moved to different contexts but instead when they are attributed to different authors. That is the point of what the narrator calls Menard's "new technique" of "erroneous attribution" (44), which prompts the narrator to consider attributing "the *Imitatio Christi* to Louis Ferdinand" (44). It is only when context refers to the context of authorship and intention that this claim works, but then context becomes just another way of talking about authorship and intention.

Borges not only emphasizes that the author's intention is what matters but also reveals that the reader—and the reader's experience—does not matter. If Borges wanted to affirm the role of the reader over the intention of the author, then the differences between Menard's *Quixote* and Cervantes's would be profoundly visible, not "invisible" as the narrator suggests. The differences would have to include any and all of the physical differences, intentional or not, between the two *Quixotes*. Without an appeal to the intention of the author of each text, the narrator would be left without a ground from which to decide what is meaningful and what is not in each text. Moreover, Menard's "new technique" of reading by means of "erroneous attribution" would make no sense, since the very question of attribution would be rendered irrelevant.

If intention is what makes the visible differences between the two texts irrelevant for Borges's narrator, it is also what makes *him* irrelevant. In the absence of the relevance of the reader, the reader's experience, or contexts, the text's meaning is fixed—indistinguishable from the author's intention, and outside of us. To put it differently, when we believe that a text means something, we also believe that it would have had that meaning even if we had never existed; alternatively, when we change our beliefs about what a text means, we conclude that our previous belief was wrong, not that it was correct given who we were and the evidence that was available to us at the time. This points to the fact that meaning is independent of our experience and the context in which we encounter the text. If that is true, then a belief about what a text means is also a belief about what it should mean for everyone. One of the frequently misunderstood aspects of the argument in "Against Theory" deals with the role beliefs play in interpretation. The fantasy of "theory," argue Knapp and Michaels, is that there can be a model for interpretation that does not involve the interpreter's beliefs (737). The idea that beliefs are essential to interpretation might lead some to conclude that true interpretations are impossible. Knapp and Michaels, however, argue that just because beliefs are subjectively produced "does not in any way weaken their claims to be true" (738). Quoting Stanley Fish, they rightly insist that if "one believes what one believes," then "one believes that what one believes is *true*" (738).

A text's meaning is thus never truly ours because what a text means is a belief about what is true outside of our experience. The fact that we can have interpretative disagreements leads us to recognize the extent to which we think that *our* interpretation is in fact *the* interpretation. The point of "Pierre Menard" is not that we do not experience texts, or that texts do not produce affective responses in us. Instead, it is that the reader's experience, affective responses, and identity are one thing, and the meaning of a text is another.

Nowhere, perhaps, is the effort to privilege a text's effects on readers over the question of its meaning more visible than in Roberto Fernández Retamar's essay "Some Theoretical Problems of Spanish-American Literature" (1974), which is one of his most sustained reflections on the politics of literary interpretation and one of the core essays in his influential book *Para una teoría de la literatura hispanoamericana* (1975). Fernández Retamar writes that, given the "dependent, precarious nature of our historical existence," it "has fallen to literature to assume functions that in the metropolises have been segregated out of it."[20] Those "functions" are political ones, and Fernández Retamar (quoting José Antonio Portuondo) affirms that the main "*constant* in the Latin-American cultural process" is the "instrumental [. . .] character" of its literature (85).[21]

Fernández Retamar thus offers a familiar account of Latin American literature's specificity: as Roberto González Echevarría notes, ideas regarding what is unique about Latin American literature have often focused not on its formal properties but on its instrumentality—specifically, its participation in "the struggle for political and cultural independence."[22] This has been viewed in both positive and negative terms.[23] In *Rubén Darío: Su personalidad literaria, su última obra* (1899), for example, José Enrique Rodó refers to the "fighting *utilitarianism*" at the heart of the Latin American literary tradition, and argues that "all manifestations of poetry in América have been more or less subjugated by the supreme necessity of propaganda and [political] action."[24] Because of Latin American literature's investment in "action," he proposes, questions of form have been rendered unimportant; when poetry "takes on the task of social struggle," Rodó declares, it cannot be "a poetry that is crafted."[25]

Mario Vargas Llosa, writing in the 1970s, argues that in Latin America being a writer was thought to mean that "you should serve, through your writing but also through your actions, as an active participant in the solution of the economic, political, and cultural problems of your society."[26] Vargas Llosa, however, finds a problem with this imperative. On the one hand, he celebrates the fact that Latin America's literature offers "the best—and sometimes the only—testimony to [. . .] our reality," but on the other hand, he complains that it has not always been "good literature" (7) because Latin American writers have "sacrificed their vocation on the altar of politics" (8). The problem for Vargas Llosa, then, is that if "creative writings are seen only (or even mainly) as the materialization of social and political aims," then those works must be judged and evaluated not in terms of their formal properties but rather in terms of their political effects—in terms of things outside the texts themselves. "How can I condemn as an artistic failure," he asks, "a novel that explicitly protests against the oppressors of the masses without being considered an accomplice of the oppressor?" (14).

Fernández Retamar's "Some Theoretical Problems of Spanish American Literature" attempts to solve this problem by collapsing Vargas Llosa's distinction between art and politics. In other words, if the problem for Vargas Llosa has to do with his simultaneous desire for both "good literature" and a literature that offers a solution to "economic, political, and cultural problems," then the solution offered by Fernández Retamar is to conflate the two sets of criteria. The question of a work's quality is thus to be answered by referring to things markedly outside of the work itself—namely, the political effects it produces. Fernández Retamar claims that the "basic precondition for understanding our literature, as Mariátegui never tired of saying, is to be found outside literature" (78). Fernández Retamar suggests that European and North American literature is often "refined by a lengthy process of distillation that [. . .] allows for an ease, a confidence, that we rarely possess" (96), whereas Latin American literature was born out of "a harsh, indeterminate reality," and since it has largely sought to change that reality, it should be evaluated in terms of its "contribution to the attainments of humankind" (96).

Fernández Retamar argues, therefore, that what is urgently needed is "our own critical outlook, our own approach to research," derived "from our own conditions, our needs, our interests" (75). Only such a "decolonized" outlook (74), he suggests, can properly understand and assess Latin American literature precisely in terms of the traits that define it, namely, its political "functions" and "concrete work" (86). Fernández Retamar argues that studying the formal properties of a text or producing a "description of a literary work's structures" is perhaps "interesting" (95), but it is ultimately useless in dealing with what really matters about a Latin American literary text—the question of its "*functional instrumentality*" (85).

Fernández Retamar rightly infers that studying a text's instrumentality has little or nothing to do with its structures or formal properties. The new "critical outlook" that Fernández Retamar proposes means ignoring the formal properties of a text in favor of looking at things outside the text, namely, its effects on readers. That is because formal properties have to do with meaning, whereas instrumentality has to do with effects. In other words, meaning is normative, whereas effects are descriptive. What we think a text means (or what we think a text is) is either right or wrong. However, the effects a text produces are just the effects it produces; as long as we recognize that not everyone is affected by it in the same way, an account of its effects will always be anchored in the identity of the reader experiencing the effects and not in the text that produced them.

Fernández Retamar's essay is on the surface an argument against what he calls "para-formalist ahistoricism" (89), and he sets out to reveal "the incongruity of approaching [Latin American literature] with intellectual tools derived from other literatures" (74). It quickly becomes clear, however, that what Fernández Retamar opposes is any interest whatsoever in form, which is to say, the idea that what matters about a text is to be found inside it. Fernández Retamar associates the impulse to think of texts in terms of their "formal experiments" with European culture and its "universality," which "we are agreed in rejecting" (79). Herein are the larger stakes of Fernández Retamar's argument: an investment in questions of form implies universalism, and the way out of that universalism is therefore the rejection of form.

Fernández Retamar is correct on this count: form has an intrinsic relationship to universalism.[27] The very identification of a text's formal properties—what they are, or even the fact that they are formal properties *as such* in the first place—is universalist. Without intention, we are unable to answer the question of what is part of the text and what is not.[28] But if what matters about a text is our experience of it, then it becomes impossible to distinguish between what is part of the text and what is not: the page numbers and the font, for example, which are undoubtedly part of our experience, cannot be excluded from the text without the claim that the author did not intend for them to be included. To be sure, it is only our belief about what an author intended that would allow us to decide, for example, that the typeface is part of the text in "painted poems" by Vicente Huidobro but not part of the text in an essay by Arturo Uslar Pietri.

In short, questions of form and meaning require beliefs about what authors have intended, and the trouble is that beliefs—including those concerning the intentions of authors—are either true or false. In terms of form and meaning, however, this implies a choice between the intention of the author and the identity of the reader. Fernández Retamar's preoccupation with forms and points of view are based on an anxiety about how form and meaning threaten the relevance of identity. Fernández Retamar condemns the investment in the formal properties of texts on the part of both literary critics and writers, and he was, of course, far from alone in this stance. Mario Benedetti, for example, once declared that "the almost fanatical interest in forms, structures, and signifiers might be a way of avoiding [. . .] the demands of the real world."[29] The interest in formal questions, argues Fernández Retamar, is the product of the "pathetic bovarism" of Latin American writers and critics who "imagine themselves as exiled metropolitans" (82). He responds to Julio Cortázar's claim that what is needed is "a Che Guevara of language" by suggesting that such an idea is "in partial agreement" with the thinking of "purely colonialized critics" who "scavenge the theoretical leftovers that fall from the West's dinner table" (94). To be interested in a Che Guevara of language is to believe that what works contain is of intrinsic note or value, and this is the very idea that Fernández Retamar wants to reject. "Che's works," writes Fernández Retamar, "belong to the main line of Spanish American literature" (which he previously defined in terms of its "*functional instru-*

mentality" [85]), and thus "the Che Guevara of language proper to our America is . . . Che Guevara" (94).

Fernández Retamar denounces "ahistoricizing criticism" or "technically 'literary'" perspectives (97) because these cannot help clarify "what separates [Latin American literature] from other literatures" (96). The task, he states, is to find a way to distinguish between "what within it [. . .] is dead weight, pastiche, the mimetic echo of metropolitan achievements" and what is our "'heroic creation,' our true contribution to the attainments of humankind" (96). Indeed, on the basis of formal properties or purely literary perspectives alone, the question of what is and is not uniquely "ours" is not easily answered.[30] Fernández Retamar freely admits as much: putting "formal" questions at the "forefront" of critical endeavors risks making Latin American literature look like "a mere projection of metropolitan culture" instead of "what it actually is" (74).

This claim helps clarify what is ultimately at stake in Sarlo's celebration of "Pierre Menard." If Borges's story suggests that all texts are equally original, then what Sarlo calls the "hierarchical order" between original and copy disappears.[31] Therefore, she argues, "in the geographical-cultural margin of the River Plate" there emerges a "new situation for the writer and for Argentine literature."[32] In other words, she writes, once the "hierarchical order attributed to originals" disappears, so, too, does "the inferiority of the margins," and "the peripheral writer is entitled to the same claims as his or her European predecessors or contemporaries."[33]

Fernández Retamar's own position, however, is far more radical: for him, what matters about a text is found outside the text in its "functions" or effects. Fernández Retamar makes form irrelevant; the analysis of a work's formal properties can at best garner our "admiration" or at worst our "indifference" (26). Indeed, if what matters is our assessment of a text's function or effects, we need not look to the text at all, but only to its readers who register those effects. In other words, we need not inquire into the meaning or working of its "structures," only into how those structures produce effects and achieve "functions."

Given that Fernández Retamar believes that Latin American literature's main task is to "express our problems and affirm our own values," the effort to replace a text's meaning with its functions not only manages to make Latin American literature "ours," but also makes it possible for *any* text to be "ours," since the crucial thing about it would be registered in terms of its specific effects on *us* (74). Moreover, the task of reading literature would first involve establishing the right "eyes with which to see it" (82). The formal properties of a text, in other words, are produced by its author, but its effects are produced by us and are thus radically and inescapably our own. If we think that a text's meaning is what its author intended, then even a text that is a representation of us will be at best what someone else saw at the moment they saw it. However, if we think that a text's meaning is bound up with the effects it produces on us (or our participation in its meaning), then a text does not need to even be a representation of us in order to be about who we are. A text, in other words, becomes a reflection of who we are in the instant we read it, and when we read it, we find ourselves confronted not with what someone else saw but with what we see.

In his critique of Eurocentric theoretical models, Fernández Retamar notes that "there are, on the other hand, books that aspire to absolute fidelity to the peculiarities of our literature of our world, but are inept in other ways" (76–77). One of these other ways involves the "urge to ontologize," as can be seen in *Historia y problemas de la literatura latinoamericana* (1972) by the German-Argentinean critic Rudolf Grossman. Fernández Retamar outlines Grossman's argument that in the regions where "blacks are dominant," certain characteristics "reign victorious," such as "a sensuality, stronger even than in the mestizo or Creole, born of a lack of self-control in their emotional life and bolstered by exuberant fantasy, a love of physical well-being, and the verbally eloquent expression of same" (77). Fernández Retamar rightly dismisses such claims as "racist aberrations" (77); indeed, Grossman's argument is that there is an essential relationship between who we are and how we write. But since Fernández Retamar has given up on trying to establish Latin American literature's distinctiveness based on the idea that its formal characteristics are different, he no longer needs the kind of essentialist relationship between identity and form offered by Grossman and others. The subject position of the reader, rather than the text, becomes the site of identitarian difference.

To see how the logic of Fernández Retamar's arguments continues to operate in Latin American literary and cultural studies today, we need look no further than Román de la Campa's *Latin Americanism* (1999). Even though de la Campa declares an interest in finding a way of doing Latin American cultural studies that can "deconstruct identitarian longings," he insists that such a project must not involve "erasing the theoretical legacies of [Latin America's] modern period."[34] Indeed, de la Campa critiques "postmodern deconstructive criticism" (12) because, he argues, it results in the "social specificity" (20) of "Latin American modernity" being "flattened or erased" (65). Thus, even though de la

Campa is skeptical about certain forms of identitarianism and what he calls the "demons of essentialism" (102), his anxieties about theory are fundamentally identitarian. In place of essentialist demons, de la Campa commits to the centrality of subject positions in a nearly literal, physical way. What matters, he argues, is "specificity in time and space" (89); the trouble with the "postmodern deconstructive" (12) theorists, he insists, is that they attempt (but can never achieve) a transcendence of "specificity in time and space." For example, he refers to the "universalist [. . .] pretense of free-floating positionality" (ix) that reduces "Latin American textuality" to a "free-floating epistemic big bang" (19), and he complains about theorists who see themselves as "free-floating scanning subject[s]" (xi), echoing Martí's admonition in "Nuestra América" that "we can no longer be a nation of fluttering leaves, spending our lives in the air."³⁵ De la Campa claims that "positionality is profoundly revealing" (42), but in fact, Latin Americanism makes positionality essential (even if not necessarily essentialized): since "specificity in time and space" is different in the here and now than it was in the there and then, de la Campa's proposed revisions to Latin Americanist literary and cultural studies practice will always involve accounting for this or that spatial-temporal specificity lest it impose the cultural logic of one spatiotemporality onto another.

Indeed, the main source of anxiety for de la Campa, as for Fernández Retamar, is not so much the specific content of certain theories but rather theory writ large, given that theories are, by their very nature as theories, universal—not in the sense of universally held but in the sense of true for everyone if true. Even a theory of particularity or difference, in order to be a theory, must make a claim of truth that transcends particularity and difference, so that when we have a theory, whatever that theory might be, we do not think that it is true for us because it happens to be our theory; rather, we think it is our theory because it is true. If de la Campa and Fernández Retamar share an anxiety about theory's intrinsic universalism, they also share a solution—namely, the creation of a hybrid theory that would fuse theories emanating from Europe and/or the United States with elements of Latin America's cultural or historical specificity.

For Fernández Retamar, quoting Jaime Labastida, this involves neither "vulgar sociologism" nor an obsession with "signifiers" and "the parole of the novelists' écriture" and is thus "the best of each method" (98). Theoretical hybridity, Fernández Retamar suggests, sidesteps the universalism implicit in theory and, by virtue of its hybridity, becomes a reflection of Latin American particularity given that—as he argued in "Caliban: Notes Toward a Discussion of Culture in Our America" (1971)—"our authentic culture" is in fact "the culture created by the mestizo populace" (36). Latin American theory should be hybrid, Fernández Retamar suggests, because Latin America is hybrid, and hybrid Latin American theories, he goes on to suggest, will make "our letters" a reflection of "our way of being in the world" (92). De la Campa, for his part, turns to Fernando Ortiz's notion of "transculturation" for the same ends. It is worth noting that, unlike Fernández Retamar, who wants Latin American literature's specificity to entail specific content—not "pastiche" or the "echo of metropolitan achievements" but rather the culture's "heroic creation" (96)—de la Campa merely wants Latin American literature to have a specificity. Fernández Retamar rejects Borges because he is a "typical colonial writer" who merely "shuffled together" and "collated" European writers (28). These same qualities, however, are why de la Campa embraces Borges.

Fernández Retamar wonders why the "American-ness of Sarmiento" is "denied to Borges" (28). Indeed, Fernández Retamar insists that Borges "is not a European writer" because "there is no European writer like Borges" (28). "Apart from a few professors of philology," he suggests, "there is only one type of person who really knows in its entirety the literature of Europe: the colonial" (28). Thus, Fernández Retamar argues that although Borges does not "represent the positive pole" of "American-ness," he nevertheless represents *a* pole of "American-ness" (28). The pole of "American-ness" that Borges represents is the reason Fernández Retamar rejects him; the fact that Borges represents any "American-ness" at all is the reason de la Campa embraces him. This is why de la Campa complains that Borges is often read by "First World philosophers and theorists" as if he were "just another European author" (34). The "uniqueness" of Borges, he argues, is found precisely in "his Latin American provenance" (34). What Fernández Retamar dismisses as "collating," de la Campa celebrates as the "liminality" that marks Borges's specificity as a Latin American—but only after he has identified Borges as a Latin American having "the standard Latin American experience with contradictory, and often foreign, teleologies" (35). Once "this culture" is defined as one "laden with ludic uncertainty" (35), then Borges becomes a mirror of "this culture" who "transcreated" this culture in his texts (35). Of course, the recognition of Borges's specificity in terms of his "liminality" is possible, de la Campa suggests, only within a theoretical framework that has liminal boundaries.

De la Campa cites Debra Castillo and Édouard Glissant, two practitioners of such a theoretical framework: Castillo claims that she develops "an applicable feminist strategy based on an infrastructure of evolved and evolving Latin American theory, while taking from first world feminist theory that which seems pertinent and complementary" (28), and Glissant writes that although there are ways in which "we actually relate to these ideas that have emerged elsewhere," ultimately "our critique of them" derives "from a burning need for modification" (116). The idea is that modifying, combining, or transculturating theory gives us a theory that is specifically ours by virtue of its emergence in a process—transculturation—that was already specifically ours since, as de la Campa argues, "long before the advent of postmodern troping, the names Frantz Fanon, Aimé Césaire, Nicolás Guillén, C. L. R. James, and Fernando Ortiz gave meaning to such categories" as "hybridity, mimicry, syncretism, and transculturation" (85). In turn, that transculturated theory not only gives us a theory that is distinctly ours but also reveals Latin America's cultural production to be the distinctive product of a time and place with its own distinctive "experience of multiple cultural entanglements" (27). Our specificity leads us to a theory that is specifically ours, de la Campa seems to argue, which in turn becomes an instrument for revealing our specificity.

Ricardo Kalimán begins his essay "Sobre la construcción del objeto en la crítica literaria latinoamericana" (1993) by noting that "some students are surprised by the doubts that were once expressed regarding the incorporation" of texts such as the chronicles of the Indies into the literary canon.[36] Kalimán points out that "there is no doubt that the very possibility of this controversy is the questioning of the very concept of literature, given its historical mutability" (308). That "questioning" leads Kalimán to the conclusion that "the category of literature is a historical construction that has fulfilled an ideological function" (311).

Moreover, the question of literary value does not follow "criteria with an empirical element" and is thus always "an act of power" (311). Even the idea of "national literature," Kalimán argues, depends not only on the unstable and constantly changing construction of the literary but also on the problematic assumption that a "given text [. . .] has certain characteristics because it was produced in the breast of this or that nation" (312). In this model the critic "adopts a priori a [homogenizing] concept of nation and proceeds to objectivize it in literary texts" and conflates these concepts with those of the state (313). Thus, Kalimán suggests, instead of "constructing" literary communities (by producing interpretations), the critic should simply "study them" (314). In effect, Kalimán argues, "if there is one thing that is clear with respect to the concept of literature, it is that it only makes sense in reference to a specific community, something which remained hidden only because criticism has traditionally attempted to 'universalize' the beliefs of its own community" (314). Thus, once we "realize that [ideas concerning what counts as literature] are historically relative, we discover" that each community is merely one "in a constellation of many communities that have existed within the frame of different societies," and therefore "our task consists of finding the theoretical instruments that will allow us to analyze the structure of those communities" (314). The study of literature, in other words, becomes radically disarticulated from the texts themselves and focused entirely on its communities of readers.

Even though Kalimán is skeptical about the identitarianism involved in the notion of national literature, his theoretical approach, which shifts attention away from the meaning of the text and toward its readings, opens the door to a more radical form of identitarianism. If the concept of national literature is problematic because it assumes that texts have specific characteristics because they were produced in a particular time and place, then Kalimán transfers that specificity onto readers in a particular time and place. Once the important questions about texts deal not with a text's formal properties but with the subject positions of its readers, the study of literature can begin to highlight the identitarian difference of readers, along with what Kalimán calls the "subindexes" of their relativity (314).

Like Kalimán, Octavio Paz seems to be questioning notions of national literatures and essences, at least in his prologue to *Poesía en movimiento: México 1915–1966* (1966), the generation-defining anthology of Mexican poetry edited by Octavio Paz, Alí Chumacero, José Emilio Pacheco, and Homero Aridjis. Paz declares that he does not "think that Mexican poetry" has "an essential character."[37] Such a declaration might seem surprising for at least two reasons. First, Paz is often associated with what has been called the "search for the true character of the Mexican people" in *The Labyrinth of Solitude* (1950).[38] Second, *Poesía en movimiento* was intended as a replacement for Antonio Castro Leal's *La poesía mexicana moderna* (1953), which up to that point had defined the canon of Mexican national poetry.[39]

Paz begins his introduction to *Poesía en movimiento* by suggesting that "the phrase *Mexican poetry* is ambiguous," especially since the "Mexicanness" of the poets included in the anthology was, he argues, "as dubious as the very idea of a national genius" (3). Anxious about the claims of national essences that might be implied by a single-nation poetry anthology, the four editors of *Poesía en movimiento* prefaced the book with a warning to readers that "this book is not, and does not want to be, an anthology" (1).[40] Indeed, the title of the anthology markedly avoided the use of "Mexican" as an adjective to describe the book's contents, opting instead for a reference to "Mexico" as the place from which the texts emerged.[41] For Paz, this functioned to underscore not only the "insufficiency" of "national criteria" (5) to describe the nature of the work produced by Mexican poets, but also the anthology's contingent status as "a fragment, the Mexican part," of a larger whole (4). Paz notes in his introduction that "it is said that López Velarde is the most Mexican of our poets," but under closer scrutiny, he argues, Ramón López Velarde's poems actually bear "more than a slight resemblance to the poetry of the Argentine [Leopoldo] Lugones, whose poems, in turn, resemble those of the Frenchman [Jules] Laforgue" (3). For Paz, "what we call national traditions are, almost always, versions and adaptations of styles that were universal," and therefore "national histories of our literature are [. . .] artificial" (4).

Thus, it might appear that Paz is abandoning a commitment to notions such as "Mexican poetry," "national genius," or the "essential character" of Mexicanness in favor of a full-blown cosmopolitanism. In fact, however, Paz is merely transferring the identitarian work of literature onto readers: Paz advances an account of meaning that is even more radically and fundamentally identitarian than the notions of national essences he repudiates. In other words, Paz rejects the idea that Mexican poetry has an "essential character," and then he affirms that meaning "is constantly changing and temporary: it springs from the interaction between the poem and the reader" (34). Paz thus produces an account of meaning that shifts the burdens of identity from "Mexican poems" onto Mexican readers. The identitarianism implied in Paz's account of meaning does not rely on any particular way of understanding identity (i.e., essentialist or performative) or its content (i.e., national, regional, locational, or cultural). In *Las corrientes literarias en la América Hispánica* (1945), for example, Pedro Henríquez Ureña wrote that Andrés Bello's *Silvas americanas* (1826) grew out of the conviction that "our poetry and our literature had to reflect our distinctive personality in an authentic voice."[42] Henríquez Ureña, of course, had definite ideas about the content of "our distinctive personality"; however, the point is that however we understand the substance of our personality, the idea that the reader has a hand in the meaning of a poem makes every text a reflection of "our distinctive personality."

Indeed, Paz is committed to the idea that meaning is the product of "the interaction between the poem and the reader" (34). He expands on this idea, by asking, "Does the work of art say something, or is it a medium through which the reader can speak?" (10). In the first instance, he argues, "the reader participates inasmuch as he receives and interprets the meaning transmitted by the text" (10). In the second instance, however, "we do something more than interpret: we directly intervene and, actually, we use the text like a trampoline" (10). All works, he suggests, "emit meaning and receive new meanings from each reader" (10). Paz thus exchanges the idea of the work of art that "say[s] something" for the idea of the work of art that is "a medium through which the reader can speak"; in the former idea, what matters is what the artist intends to say, but in the latter idea, what matters is who we are, since the variation of meanings in a text will be reducible to the differences between each reader who encounters it and speaks through it. In so doing, Paz frees poetry from an older identitarian burden only to ensnare it in a new and more radical one borne by a reader who "directly intervenes" in, rather than interprets, what a text means (12). Readers, Paz argues, "are equally authors" (6), and as a result every reading bears the identitarian mark of the reader in a fundamental way, since what the text means will literally be of his or her making. Because all works will "receive new meanings from each reader," the question of what a text means will have to refer to the reader who is attributing "new meanings" to the text (10). In fact, Paz admits as much in his essay "Signs in Rotation" (1965), where he writes that "the question that the poem asks itself—who is he who says this that I say, and to whom is it said?—embraces the poet and the reader."[43]

In fact, it could be said that Paz recognizes an identitarian insufficiency in the accounts of meaning in which the reader is not a participant. Criticism, writes Paz, "almost always affirms that texts remain the same," even if "the point of view of one critic is different than another's" (6). However, Paz writes, *Poesía en movimiento* was "inspired by a different idea," namely, that "texts are never the same" (6) because they are always "in motion" (13). According to Paz, whereas classical art was "closed," modern art is "open" (10), and he goes on to argue that "modern poetry and open text are equivalent terms" (11). What distinguishes his generation from that of Borges and Neruda, he suggests, "is not only style but also the very conception of language and text" (12). For Paz, the "key word" for that conception of language is "indeterminacy" (13), which explains the idea of *movimiento* or "motion" in the anthology's title.

Crucial to "indeterminacy" is what Paz called, in one of his own poems anthologized in *Poesía en movimiento*, the abolishment of "the distance between the word and the thing" (259).⁴⁴ In *The Bow and the Lyre* (1956), Paz had already called for a "reunion" of "the word and the object, the name and the thing named," and this "reunion," he suggests, can help bring about "man's [. . .] reconciliation with himself and with the world."⁴⁵ Indeed, Paz's account of language is one in which "the distance between the word and the object [. . .] which obliges each word to become a metaphor of the thing it designates" is "the result of another distance: as soon as man acquired consciousness of himself, he broke away from the natural world and made himself another world inside himself."⁴⁶ Thus, Paz argues, the reunion between "the word and the object" will help "man [. . .] find out what he is, profoundly and originally" (26).

The transformation of signs into objects does indeed bring us closer to the question of who we are: we interpret texts, but we experience objects. Paz seems to acknowledge the difference between interpretation and experience when he suggests that even though "the point of view of one critic is different from another's," all critics tend to assume (wrongly, in his view) that "what they are looking at is the same" (6). Of course, two critics who disagree about a text nonetheless believe that they are looking at the same text even though they are looking at literally different objects. What makes this possible, Paz correctly senses, is that the "what" of "what they are looking at" is a text and not an object (if people actually thought that the materiality of "what they are looking at" was in any way relevant to their interpretation, the commonplace notion of having read the same book as someone else would be at best a rare occurrence). However, two people looking at identical but different objects that are not texts or representations could hardly imagine themselves to be seeing the same thing—they would just be seeing different objects. For Paz, then, the desire to join "the word and the object" is a precondition not only for thinking that texts are in "motion" through time and space (and from reader to reader) but also for thinking that texts can help "man" find out "what he is." If we all see the same texts, they can hardly reflect our identity; if texts are reimagined as objects, they are never exactly "the same," and how we experience them as objects will always differ depending on who we are, or where, or when, or in what context we encounter them.⁴⁷ Indeed, in an essay on William Carlos Williams, Paz suggests that "meaning ceaselessly undermines the poem" because "it seems to reduce its reality as an object of the senses [. . .] to an idea, a definition, or 'message,'" thus acknowledging the opposition between experience—"the senses"—and "meaning" (159).

To be sure, the desire to think of texts as objects is closely related to the desire to think of them in terms of their affective powers. In *Writing in the Air: Heterogeneity and the Persistence of Oral Tradition in Andean Literatures* (1994), for example, the idea of the materiality of the text is crucial for Antonio Cornejo Polar's "broad concept of literature that assumes a complete circuit of literary production, including the reception of the message."[48] Cornejo Polar begins by affirming a difference in Latin American literature itself, which proves the insufficiency of "classical philological instruments" to study it (13). But Cornejo Polar goes even further: by replacing "the book's signifying function" with its status as an "object," he produces a logic in which the experience of the reader is the only thing that counts (21).

In similar fashion, Walter Mignolo writes in *The Darker Side of the Renaissance: Literacy, Territoriality, and Colonization* (1995) that "representation is a notion I have tried to avoid as much as possible in my argument."[49] The trouble with representation, Mignolo suggests, is that it "rests on a denotative philosophy of language according to which names represent things and maps represent territories" and, as such, presupposes the possibility of people knowing "a world outside themselves" (333).[50] Mignolo associates the idea that people can know "a world outside themselves" with hierarchies of culture and knowledge. For example, Mignolo argues, "a twentieth-century observer can surmise, when comparing an illuminated medieval codex or a wonderful Renaissance book to a painted Mexica codex, that while the latter is a piece to be admired, it cannot be put at the same level as the medieval codex" (334). However, if we look at the books not as representations or "visible signs" but rather as "cultural objects" that result from "human needs" and should be judged only in relation to those needs, then the hierarchical relation disappears (334). The objects cease to have meaning and are only read in terms of their participation in "activities" between individuals or groups. In other words, Mignolo reveals that cultural (or epistemic) dehierarchization, the replacement of the intention of the author with the participation of the reader, and the interest in the materiality of the text are all related forms of the same theoretical and political effort.[51]

Whereas Mignolo and others have sought to sidestep the indifference to identity involved in interpretation by thinking of texts as objects, Doris Sommer celebrates representations that have nothing to represent. Indeed, Sommer's *Proceed with Caution, When Engaged by Minority Writing in the Americas* (1999) is one of the most influential recent attempts to theorize a way out of the universalist implications of meaning in favor of an account of reading in which identitarian difference might matter. Sommer seeks to establish a way of reading texts that would make identity matter and force readers to confront identitarian difference in a fundamental, irreducible way. Sommer argues that what she calls "resistant texts" demand to be read differently than others.[52] Reading these "ethnically marked" (xi) texts, Sommer argues, involves learning to "listen properly" for meanings that are deliberately withheld and instances where writers decidedly refuse to be understood (77). For Sommer, these instances force readers to confront not only their difference vis-à-vis the text and its author but also the limits of their ability to understand otherness. However, the idea of listening "properly" points toward one of the central contradictions in Sommer's argument.[53] That is to say, Sommer does not seek an alternative to authorial intention—on the contrary, her project fundamentally depends on it.

Sommer highlights how what she calls "particularist authors" (xii) create "an impassable distance between reader and text [. . .] thereby raising questions of access or welcome" and producing "constraints that more reading will not overcome" (8). Unlike texts that allow readers who "feel entitled to know everything as they approach a text [. . .] with the conspiratorial intimacy of a potential partner," so-called "particularist texts" are "uncooperative books" that prevent readers from pressing for the surrender of "cultural difference for the sake of universal meaning" (ix). If "learning" about a text, as Sommer argues, "makes the distance between writers and readers seem superficial or circumstantial," then particularist writing "puts circumstance to work, resurfacing the stretch and marking it with stop signs" (x). In fact, Sommer finds in "particularist writing" an effort to "propose something different from knowledge," something that might be called "acknowledgment," she suggests, or even "respect" (xi).

To be sure, one of the main goals of *Proceed with Caution* is to rethink reading practices that "forget how positionality affects knowledge" (9). Sommer claims that "asking about the place from which one speaks, the locus of enunciation, is a question sometimes put to narrators and characters, but hardly ever to readers" (9).[54] Traditional practices of reading, she argues, emphasize "understanding," which is a problem because "the will to understand can become willfulness or greed in the guise of an embrace" (27). For Sommer, then, a reader's understanding of a text cancels out not only the difference between multiple readers but also the difference between the reader and the text. The claim to understand, Sommer argues, reduces "otherness to sameness" and entails the notion that "difference is a superable problem, rather than a source of pride or simply the way we are in the world" (19). Understanding a text, in other words, "squeezes out difference, to make partners equal insofar as they are the same" (19) and engages in the fantasy that "asymmetrical relationships [can be] flattened out on the smooth surface of print culture" (xiii).

Hence the value Sommer places on "minority writing," which is characterized by absences, refusals, silences, and other kinds of "no trespassing signs that suggest cautious approaches" (31). Given that "minority" texts contain "textual differences" that also function as "markers of the political differences that keep democracy interesting and honest" (4), Sommer calls for a "paradigm shift" so that readers might begin to notice the signs that mark off the political and aesthetic resistance "minority writing" contains (31).

Sommer writes that *Proceed with Caution* began in part after she read Rigoberta Menchú's *testimonio* (115). "Her secrets stopped me then," Sommer writes, "and instruct me now in other contexts, whatever the validity of the information or the authenticity of the informant" (115). The "validity of the information" is irrelevant because the power of Menchú's *testimonio* is supposedly located in its *refusal* to "share information" and its "secrets" (115).

Sommer's attempt to find a practice of reading capable of protecting "our foreignness" and "our cultural difference" by making "secrets incomprehensible" ends up intensifying a commitment to the idea that what a text means is only what its author intends, which in turn negates the value she places on textual secrets, silences, and refusals (122). Sommer, for example, repeatedly refers to "deliberate silence" (171), "intentional absences" (24), selective rhetoric, "purposeful incomprehensibility" (15), and "creative refusals to talk" (21). Indeed, Sommer's project depends on the idea that the silences and absences are what "resistant authors *intend*" (8). Sommer approvingly quotes Stanley Cavell (from *Must We Mean What We Say?*), stating that even formalists (beginning with Kant) saw "'purposiveness' in art" (8). To be sure, Sommer must concede that "resistant authors intend to produce constraints that more reading will not overcome" (8). Refusal of meaning is the point in the texts she discusses as well as what gives them their political force, since the difference between withholding information and neglecting to reveal information is predicated on intentionality.

What Sommer wants to do away with is the supposed illusion of textual mastery that allows readers to think they can know everything that is meant by a text. Sommer calls for a new reading practice that can recognize the silences and absences that are politically and textually meaningful because the author intended them to be there. However, it is hard to see how properly reading silences that the author intended counts as a new way of reading or an alternative to the concept of textual mastery. If "limited access is the point" (8), then properly grasping "limited access" *as* "limited access" involves grasping the totality of its meaning. In other words, since the only thing to grasp is that there is nothing to grasp—the author's intention to be silent—then all that remains is authorial intention itself. Fully grasping the text, or "mastering" it, to use Sommer's words, is achieved by realizing that someone intended for there to be nothing there for us to master. Sommer's claim that the crucial work of the text comes in the form of what it refuses to represent brings us back to the notion of mastery and complete knowledge that *Proceed with Caution* set out to repudiate. *Proceed with Caution* ultimately reveals the inescapability of the point made by Borges in "Pierre Menard": a text means what its author intended it to mean.

It is worth recalling, in conclusion, that in *Subalternity and Representation: Arguments in Cultural Theory* (1999), John Beverley refers to Borges's "overtly reactionary politics" and wonders whether "those politics" are "related to his function as a storyteller as well."[55] Borges gives us both a politics and, at least in "Pierre Menard," a much-needed logic by which we can disagree with those politics and reject them.

CHAPTER FOUR

Memory

*I*N HIS 1987 BOOK *MÉXICO PROFUNDO: RECLAIMING a Civilization*, the anthropologist Guillermo Bonfil Batalla complained that the Mexican middle class had no "desire to remember" the "precolonial world."[1] By suggesting that the middle class—and other members of what he referred to as the "imaginary Mexico"—had no interest in remembering the precolonial world, Bonfil did not mean to imply that the precolonial world was unknown. In fact, Bonfil acknowledged not only that "every schoolchild knows something about the precolonial world" (3) but also that the precolonial world was "depicted in murals, museums, [and] sculptures" (55).[2] Moreover, he added, "the great archaeological monuments stand as national symbols," and Mexicans take "pride in a past that is [. . .] assumed to be glorious" (3). Bonfil thus was not using the concept of memory as shorthand for knowledge. On the contrary, Bonfil believed that the difference between "imaginary Mexico" and *"México profundo"* was reducible in part to two different ways of relating to the past: whereas "imaginary Mexico" had no "desire to remember," *'México profundo'* actually "remember[s] history" (35). As a result, when Bonfil wrote that one of his aims was to "point toward a way of thinking about our history" (69), what he meant was thinking about it not as history but rather as memory.

Leaving aside the fact that it is hard to understand how someone who was alive in 1987 could remember the precolonial past, we can begin to understand why Bonfil would have wanted the precolonial past to be remembered rather than known. In order for the precolonial past to function as what he called a "mirror in which [. . .] to see our own reflection" (18), we must think of it not as "something apart from ourselves" but rather as "our own past" since, as Bonfil seemed to imply, history is about "*them*," whereas memory is about "*us*" (3). However, before the precolonial past can become "our own past" that we remember rather than "something that happened long ago" that we learn about, we have to imagine a way for the past to reemerge in the present as something that we can actually experience (3).[3] This, at least in part, explains why Bonfil insisted that the precolonial past should be seen as "present and alive" (174) rather than "dead" (3). It also clarifies, at least in part, why Bonfil was committed to the idea of the "continuity of Mesoamerican civilization" (62), enabled by the "persistence of the peoples who preserved it and brought it into the present" (159). Indeed, the idea that indigenous cultural practices in the present are aspects of the precolonial past that have been "brought [. . .] into the present" is what is needed in order to think that the precolonial past can be remembered rather than known.

Bonfil's enthusiasm for a remembered history belonged to a broader turn in Latin Americanist thought in which memory began to take the place of culture in conceptions of Latin American identity. The preservation and assertion of Latin American identitarian difference has been thought, at least since the late nineteenth century, to constitute the cornerstone of a politics of resistance. The substance of that difference, of course, was traditionally thought to be cultural. If, however, beginning in the 1980s, globalization seemed to threaten the persistence of cultural difference, one of the solutions generated by Latin Americanist thought was to locate identitarian difference in a remembered history so that cultural difference in the past could constitute the identitarian difference of people in the present.[4] If the imperative in foundational nineteenth-century Latin Americanist texts such as José Martí's "Nuestra América" (1891) was for Latin Americans to actually *practice* a supposedly indigenous or autochthonous culture, the vital message beginning in the 1980s was that they should *remember* it. A variety of theoretical projects—such as performance—followed suit to make those memories possible, either by imagining ways to make the past alive in the present (so that it could be experienced and remembered), or by imagining technologies that could, as Diana Taylor says of performance, "transmit" memory.[5]

Memory projects have been not only theoretical but also political: Bonfil's *México Profundo* was published toward the end of a decade that in Mexico was characterized by a large-scale financial crisis resulting in the first wave of neoliberal economic reforms, falling wages, unemployment, and rapidly increasing income inequality.[6] Bonfil, for his part, noted that "the crisis has made the rich richer and everyone else poorer" (155) and suggested that a renewed or recovered relationship to Mesoamerican civilization could offer a politics of resistance and "repair the damages produced by a savage capitalism" (156). More recently, Sandra Lorenzano has suggested that "if economic neoliberalism has counteracted any labor or social development in the region," or if "social fabrics have unraveled with profound losses in human and civil rights," then "memory is one of the only remaining spaces of resistance."[7] If the turn toward memory was understood to be both theoretical and political, the trouble here is that it entailed bad theories and an even worse politics. It might be said that the problem with the politics of memory is that it emphasizes an affective identification with people in the past at the expense of a class-based identification with people in the present. However, the real problem with the politics of memory is that it seeks to keep intact not only the idea that identitarian difference is the cornerstone of resistance, but also the idea that the meaningful differences between people are identitarian ones that should be preserved through memory rather than economic ones that should be eliminated through politics. The fact that the rise of the discourse of memory coincided with the rise of neoliberalism, in other words, should lead us to see memory as an epiphenomenon of neoliberalism rather than a mode of resistance to it.[8]

The articulation and production of cultural difference has been central to the project of Latin Americanism. The ideas about culture and difference articulated in José Martí's "Nuestra América" became a Latin Americanist orthodoxy that has been articulated in a diverse body of influential writings, such as Rubén Darío's "A Roosevelt" (1904), José Carlos Mariátegui's *Seven Interpretative Essays on Peruvian Reality* (1928), Nicolás Guillén's *Sóngoro cosongo* (1931), and Roberto Fernández Retamar's "Caliban: Notes Toward a Discussion of Culture in Our America" (1971).

As Carlos Alonso has argued, given that Latin American cultural discourse was predicated on the conviction that the desired culture was "consubstantial with the community," its recoverability was "always [. . .] portrayed as an imminent achievement."[9] In other words, the assumption was that it "never *really* left there in the first place" (12). In "Nuestra América," for example, Martí wrote that the "Indian circled about us," but was "mute"; the black man "sang his heart's music in the night," but was "alone and unknown."[10] In *Forjando patria* (1916), Manuel Gamio declared that the "Mayas of Quintana Roo, like the Lacandónes of Chiapas, the Maya of the Petén, and a few other groups [. . .]

live in almost the same state in which their ancestors were surprised by the Conquest."¹¹ Guillén's prologue to *Sóngoro cosongo* identified a crisis of African culture in Cuba, only to then affirm the inescapable persistence of *afrocubanidad* through biology: the "African injection in this land is so profound, and so many capillary currents cross and crisscross in our well-irrigated social hydrography."¹² In his *Seven Interpretative Essays on Peruvian Reality*, despite the claims that "the conquest most clearly appears to be a break in continuity," or that colonization brought about the "disappearance" of an indigenous economy "together with the culture it nourished," Mariátegui affirmed "the survival of the Indian 'community' and of elements of practical socialism in indigenous agriculture and life."¹³ And in 1979, Octavio Paz wrote that in Mexico, "the old beliefs [. . .] are still present, barely hidden under a veneer of Christianity."¹⁴ Paz added, "The Mexicans' entire life is steeped in Indian culture—the family, love, friendship, attitudes toward one's father and mother, popular legends, the forms of civility and life in common, the image of authority and political power, the vision of death and sex, work and festivity."¹⁵

By the 1980s, confidence in the persistence of Latin American cultural difference was shaken by the increasing dominance of globalized U.S. culture. As Jorge Larrain suggests, by "the end of the 1980s [. . .] the project of rapidly advancing to modernity, even at the cost of identity, was becoming dominant in Latin America."¹⁶ Larrain goes on to argue that "the stage that opens up after the end of dictatorships [in the 1980s] continues with, and accelerates, economic and political modernization under the influence of an already consolidated neoliberal ideology"; the result is that "concerns about [Latin American autochthonous] identity recede as neoliberal optimism gets the upper hand everywhere."¹⁷ In a 1994 interview with Claire Brewster, Carlos Monsiváis reflected on the 1988 election of Carlos Salinas to the Mexican presidency, which began a period of neoliberal economic reforms culminating in the ratification of NAFTA on January 1, 1994. Monsiváis stated that it was "an incredible time" because many Mexicans seemed to think, "'Wow, we've made it, for the first time we're joining the First World.'"¹⁸ During a time when some prominent intellectuals championed neoliberal reforms, many others grew anxious about the possibility of Latin American difference represented in, or constituted by, actual cultural practices. Whereas in 1916 Gamio claimed that "75 percent" of the population of Latin America was "composed of men of [. . .] indigenous language, and indigenous civilization," in 2001 Néstor García Canclini observed that the "aesthetic taste" of Mexicans was heavily influenced by U.S. films, which had a 60–85 percent market share in all venues: movie houses, television, and video.[19]

If some Latin Americanist thought in the 1980s was anxious about the possibility of preserving Latin American difference constituted by culture, the commitment to difference itself remained intact. The new challenge for Latin Americanist thought was to find ways to preserve the idea of Latin American difference without the cultural practices that would constitute the substance of that difference. One major strategy that emerged was to locate identity and difference in history, and to find ways to make history constitute part of the experience and thus the identity of people who had not lived through it in the first place. Latin Americanist thought turned to memory when it gave up on Latin American culture—but not on the identitarian difference that was constituted or represented by that culture. In this way, memory functioned to radically separate identity and culture, so that identity could be thought of as no longer dependent on, or derived from, cultural practices in the present.

To see the extent to which memory performs the function previously of older forms of identity, we need look no further than Jeanette Rodríguez and Ted Fortier's *Cultural Memory: Resistance, Faith, and Identity* (2007). In the introduction, the authors write that "'sangre llama a sangre' (blood calls to blood) is an expression or metaphor that alludes to blood as the carrier of one's life, which is in turn connected to others."[20] Moreover, they add, blood "is the life force that allows one access to the affective, intuitive bond of community that surges up without any rigid or rational trappings."[21] Thus, they write, "cultural memory" is in fact "blood calling out to blood."[22]

One of neoliberalism's main assumptions, as Manfred Steger and Ravi Roy have pointed out, is that single global "markets and consumerist principles are universally applicable because they appeal to all (self-interested) human beings regardless of their social context."[23] In this sense, (cultural) difference might appear to be an obstacle to creating consumers and workers within and for a global market. However, here we see one of the contradictions of neoliberalism, inasmuch as neoliberalism also requires identitarian accounts of (noneconomic) difference. One of the main strategies of neoliberalism, as Walter Benn Michaels has persuasively argued, is to give poor people "identities" in place of classes, so that they can be treated as "victims of discrimination" rather than of exploitation.[24] In other words, Michaels argues, neoliberalism is fundamentally committed to redescribing "the material difference between people [. . .] as cultural difference" in order to perpetuate the illusion that "as long as people get to keep on speaking their own languages [. . .] there's no reason for alarm."[25] Charles R. Hale argues that the rise of the official and institutionalized recognition of cultural difference perfectly coincides with neoliberalism. Hale notes that the assumption that the "victories of indigenous cultural rights" keep "the devastating effects of neoliberalism at bay" is "misleading" because "proponents of the neoliberal doctrine pro-actively endorse a substantive, if limited, version of indigenous cultural rights, as a means to resolve their own problems and political agendas."[26] For example, "in the same initiative of constitutional reform in 1992 the Mexican state recognized the 'pluri-cultural character' of the society (article 4), and eliminated the cornerstone of the revolution's historic agrarian reform (article 27)."[27] Neoliberalism is thus about "simultaneous cultural affirmation and economic marginalization."[28] But the seemingly paradoxical point is that even though actual cultural practices get in the way of neoliberalism's agenda for global consumer and labor markets, the general idea of identitarian difference does not—in fact, it is desired. Neoliberalism needs a noneconomic vocabulary for thinking about difference in order to obfuscate the economic differences—which is to say, inequalities—that it creates.

Memory, by attempting to preserve the idea of Latin American difference in the face of the disappearing cultural practices that used to be thought to constitute that difference, thus serviced the contradictory demands of the neoliberal project. Memory de-emphasized culture as the basis for Latin American difference while simultaneously functioning as a mechanism for affirming that there was such a thing as Latin American difference in the first place—only this time constituted by a remembered history. The advocates of neoliberalism themselves explicitly championed this idea: when Jaime Serra Puche (Carlos Salinas's secretary of commerce and industrial development) was asked whether NAFTA would negatively affect traditional Mexican culture, he famously replied, "This has little relevance for Mexico. If you have time, you should see the exhibition 'Mexico, Thirty Centuries of Splendor,' and you will realize there is no cause for concern."[29] Serra Puche thus refocuses a question about cultural identity in the present onto culture in the past, implying that Mexicans will always have an identity because of their history.

In the 1960s, people's memories of things they actually experienced were seen as important resources for correcting ostensibly inaccurate or incomplete accounts of the past. In this sense, memory was understood in terms of a project that entailed turning memory into history. In 1963, the Cuban scholar José Antonio Portuondo declared that up to that point, there had been "no history among us that did not study the rise and fall of the dominant hegemonic class: the [Cuban] bourgeoisie."[30] What was needed, Portuondo argued, was a history of "the exploited classes" and "their constant struggles."[31] Texts such as Miguel Barnet's *Biography of a Runaway Slave* (1966), a "novela-testimonio" based on the personal memories of former slave Esteban Montejo (1860–1973), initially appeared to fulfill that imperative by offering glimpses of a past that had been ignored or overlooked by official history or that would be unknowable through conventional archival sources. In 1971, Elena Poniatowska's oral history *Massacre in Mexico* used a great many eyewitness accounts to counter the Mexican government's cover-up of its violent attack on student protesters and bystanders on October 2, 1968, in the Plaza de las Tres Culturas in the Tlatelolco section of Mexico City. Although the fragmentary nature of *Massacre in Mexico* might suggest a skepticism on the author's part about what Beth Jörgensen calls "the homogenizing tendencies of much conventional journalism," opting instead for a "decentered, collective retelling of history," the project as a whole embraces individual memory as an effective way to correct errors and omissions in official versions of the past.[32]

By the early 1980s, the value of memory as a source for history increased as people tried to learn about and document, in the absence of other kinds of records, the political abuses and human rights atrocities committed by Argentina's military regime. The 1984 report of Argentina's National Commission on the Disappearance of Persons (CONADEP), for example, affirmed the important role that memory had played in its findings. Ernesto Sábato, who chaired the commission, remarked in his prologue upon the "arduous task" CONADEP had faced in piecing together "a shadowy jigsaw, years after the events had taken place, when all the clues had been deliberately destroyed, all documentary evidence burned, and buildings demolished."[33] The basis for CONADEP's findings, Sábato pointed out, had been "the statements made by relatives or by those who managed to escape from this hell."[34] In the case of disappeared persons, memory, rather than "documentary evidence," was often all that was available to attest that a missing person had ever even existed in the first place, since the regimes frequently destroyed all official records and physical traces of a person's existence. "The idea," as Diana Taylor rightly puts it, "was that by disappearing the documentary evidence of a human life one could erase all traces of the life itself" (63).

The publication of the 1984 CONADEP report was one of the signs that marked the rise of memory as an accepted source for knowing about the truth of the past in Latin America. Indeed, Emilio Crenzel argues that CONADEP was the first of several "truth commissions" across the region whose "reports became the main vehicles for the construction of historical truth."[35] Kerwin Klein points out that when "historians began professionalizing in the nineteenth century, they commonly identified memories as a dubious source for the verification of historical facts."[36] Written documents, on the other hand, "seemed less amenable to distortion and thus preferable to memories."[37] But the CONADEP report overcame this by asserting that memories could offer historical facts and truth: the report was interested in turning memory into history. As Crenzel argues, the individual testimony in the report became "a chorus of testimonies that transcends the partiality of personal experience and, at the same time, confirms its truthfulness through the voices of others" (1070). The report also presented "other forms of validating the facts" that confirmed the testimonies: it incorporated "scientific knowledge" that ratified "the veracity of direct experience," and cited "international science institutions" that validated the use of the report's techniques and methods (1070). Finally, the report validated its own narrative "by presenting a detailed account of its work, the interviews it conducted, the visits to clandestine centers, cemeteries, morgues, and hospitals, the trips it made to gather reports, and the cases it brought before the courts" (1071). The claim of "truth" not only made it possible for the report to install what Crenzel calls "a new official truth" (1073), but also allowed the report to function as a key piece of evidence "during the trial that led to the conviction of the military juntas" (1063). In the wake of this politically powerful harnessing of memory, as Emilia Viotti da Costa has argued, "the number of practitioners of oral history grew, as did the number of [scholarly] studies based exclusively on testimonies and interviews," and oral history began to displace "archival research."[38] At the same time, Viotti da Costa suggests, many wanted to foreground subjectivity to the point that history became merely "a confusion of subjectivities and voices."[39] Of course, the idea that all accounts of the past are necessarily subjective and contingent might be bad news for a historian seeking a truth of the past that transcends subject positions. However, for many scholars of literary and cultural studies who were seeking ways for history to give people an identity, the same idea was good news. For if we give up on the notion that there is a truth about the past and replace it with the notion that there are multiple truths about the past, then the past that is individually or communally ours becomes a marker of our difference.

José Rabasa's account of the Acteal massacre offers a clear vision of this idea at work. On December 22, 1997, forty-five members of a Christian pacifist group named "Las Abejas" were massacred in a chapel in the Chiapan village of Acteal. Conflicting accounts of what happened quickly emerged. The residents of Acteal, some of whom witnessed the events, claimed that Las Abejas fell victim to state-supported paramilitary forces because of their support for the EZLN (Ejército Zapatista de Liberación Nacional). Others corroborated their claims; for example, retired army brigadier general Julio César Santiago Díaz testified that the paramilitary forces were "accompanied by 40 state police officers" who were "stationed at the entrance to the village."[40] However, the official Mexican government account of the massacre, produced by the Mexican attorney general's office in 1998, denied any responsibility and attributed the event to "mutual grievances" that resulted from "the accumulated offences [. . .] in the indigenous communities of the region."[41]

In an essay from his book *Without History: Subaltern Studies, the Zapatista Insurgency, and the Specter of History* (2010), Rabasa considers the competing claims about what happened at Acteal. Rabasa focuses on what he calls a "revisionist" series of articles entitled "Regreso a Acteal," in which the Mexican journalist Hector Aguilar Camín supports the official government findings, characterizing the events at Acteal "as the collateral violence of a battle [. . .] between Zapatistas and Priístas."[42] Rabasa rightly believes that truth is on the side of Las Abejas, but he is ultimately less concerned with what really happened than with challenging "a historical framework that seeks to destroy the face of testimony" (232). Rather than seek the truth about the massacre, Rabasa shifts to another crime—the "assassination of memory" committed by revisionist accounts like Aguilar Camín's (237). For Rabasa, the problem is not only that Aguilar Camín lets the government of Ernesto Zedillo off the hook for a massacre, but also that his writing "strikes at the core of the Abejas' identity" (232).

Rabasa claims to explore a "disputed truth" only to give up on the idea that there is such a thing as "truth" (234). He seeks to reframe "disputed truths" in terms other than "those based on fact and falsification," which is to say, truth and falsity (236). The result is that the competing accounts of what happened at Acteal are reimagined as a conflict over identity—the "revisionists," he suggests, want to destroy it, but

Las Abejas wants to preserve it. Rabasa rejects the idea that "testimony holds an unquestionable epistemological privilege" (235); testimony, he argues, "must be suspected of manipulation when claiming [. . .] objective truth" (234). However, Rabasa argues that when testimony is freed from questions of truth—when we acknowledge that it "partakes of other forms of knowledge" (236)—it can give us identity in the place of truth.

For Rabasa, the "revisionist histories" are not merely an "assassination of memory" but an entirely new round of murders that are "beyond the act of putting to death" (237). The death they seek, in his view, is the death of the difference between the multiple accounts of the "disputed truth." The difference between the claims of Las Abejas and those of the revisionists is to be understood not as the difference between truth and falsity, or "fact and falsification," but as the difference between identities. For the beliefs of either Las Abejas *or* the revisionists to be right is to cancel the difference between them and "kill" someone's identity (237). When we disagree, we commit to the idea that our beliefs are not only true for us given our identity but also true for everyone, whatever their identity. This is why we disagree in the first place: disagreeing with others requires us to think that our beliefs are ours because we believe they are true rather than true because they are ours. If, however, we think that having a belief makes it true for the person who believes it, then disagreement becomes impossible. Without truth and falsity, we cannot claim that our beliefs are true, only that they are true for us, given who we are. Therefore, in order to explain and justify the beliefs we have, we will have to account for who we are. This is precisely what is at stake in Rabasa's "redefinition of epistemological terms" that would no longer refer to questions of truth (236). If the CONADEP report validated memory by suggesting its possible relation to truth, then Rabasa and others have sought to exempt memory from questions of truth so that memory could do identitarian work. For this reason, memory came to stand in for any and every kind of knowledge about the past.

One of the most prominent critics of the proliferation of memories and subjectivities has been Beatriz Sarlo. In *Tiempo pasado* (2005), she controversially challenges what she saw as the tendency to regard memory as an unquestioned—and unquestionable—source of truth about the past. In particular, Sarlo complains about "the transformation of *testimonio* into an icon of truth," which results from "the privileging of subjective discourses over those where subjectivity is absent or hidden."[43] Even though "memory can function as a moral challenge to history and its sources," Sarlo argues, "this cannot support memory's claims to be less problematic than what is constructed by other discourses" (57). For Sarlo, memory is part of a larger "subjective turn" in historical thinking that began when "historians and social scientists" who were "influenced by ethnography" (17) began to focus on individual subjectivities and write "histories of everyday life" (19). Even though studies such as Richard Hoggart's *The Uses of Literacy* rely on oral history and focus on individual subjectivity, such studies, Sarlo suggests, at least contain a commitment to what she called "disciplinary rules" and "methods" (14). These "methods of disciplinary history" (14) matter for Sarlo because they keep historians focused on "writing better history" and not on the market; "non-academic history," on the other hand, merely responds to "the contemporary social imaginary, whose pressure it receives and accepts more as an advantage than a limitation" (15). Sarlo sees "good academic history" (16) as something that, unlike memory, *testimonio*, and the "subjective turn," makes it possible to imagine thinking *"outside experience"* so that "humans might take control of nightmares and not merely suffer through them" (166).

Not surprisingly, it was Sarlo's belief in the value of "good academic history" that made John Beverley count *Tiempo pasado* as part of a "neoconservative turn in Latin American literary and cultural criticism."[44] For Beverley, Sarlo's *Tiempo pasado* should be understood as part of a broader attempt by a "middle and upper middle class, university-educated, and essentially white, criollo-ladino intelligentsia to recapture the space of cultural and hermeneutic authority" from the neoliberal market and from new populist political and cultural actors no longer beholden to "a university-educated, ethnically European or mestizo intelligentsia" (79). Sarlo's "good academic history" is, of course, part and parcel of what Beverley once thought *testimonio* could dismantle: *testimonio*, he wrote, "acts in the world as a regime of truth that operates 'off campus,' so to speak."[45] For Beverley, "what testimonio requires of the academy is not that we 'know' it adequately, but something like a critique of academic knowledge as such. That critique [. . .] would point in the direction of relativizing the authority of academic knowledge" and "would allow us to recognize what academic knowledge is in fact: not *the* truth, but *a form of truth*, among many others."[46]

Beverley takes issue with Sarlo not because of what she privileges as truth but because she privileges truth in the first place. Beverley thinks there are only forms of truth, never universal ones, and therefore any claim to truth is always a power grab by the particular. Neoconservatism, as Beverley understands it, entails "a hierarchy of values embedded in Western Civilization" (66). The problem, he argues, is that neo-conservatives such as Sarlo "speak *as* intellectuals in the name of the universal" (66). The real crux of the disagreement between Beverley and Sarlo is that Sarlo thinks beliefs have to come from nowhere to be true, whereas Beverley thinks they always come from somewhere, which is why they are not true. But positions such as Beverley's actually require all of us to produce accounts of our identity to justify our beliefs, since if different things are true for different people, then we must know who we are in order to know what is true for us. Beverley's call for a plurality of truths is just another way of affirming identity and protecting difference from the universalism intrinsic to beliefs. This would seem to be exactly what Sarlo points out and critiques in *Tiempo pasado*: the old battles over history, she says, "are now called battles over identity" (27). What we are left with, Sarlo argues, is only "the primacy of the subject" (27).

The difference between Sarlo and Beverley, however, is in the end more apparent than real. What Sarlo values about "good academic history" turns out to be its commitment to hypothesis over the supposed certainty she sees in self-validating and self-authorizing testimonial narratives based on memory. Accounts of the past, for Sarlo, are "always constructions" (13), and she values ways of doing history that confront the idea that "the very idea of truth is a problem" (163). Sarlo relies on Paul de Man's 1979 essay, "Autobiography as De-facement," which she calls the "highest point of literary deconstruction," arguing that de Man's claims are still unheeded by those who "affirm the truth of the subject and of autobiographical *testimonios*" (40). De Man's point, of course, was that autobiography was prosopopoeic: instead of assuming "the life produces the autobiography," the "autobiographical project may itself produce and determine the life."[47] Sarlo also refers to Jacques Derrida's idea of "otobiographies," with which he suggests that it is the "ear of the other that says me to me and constitutes the *autos* of my autobiography."[48] Sarlo invokes Derrida and de Man to make a familiar point: our knowledge of the past is *mediated*—by language, genre, reading, and so forth. For Sarlo, this is a challenge not only for those who believe memory and *testimonio* to be true, but also for historians who claim truth for their histories.

However, the claim that our knowledge or beliefs are mediated has no logical consequences unless we believe in the possibility of an *un*mediated knowledge. Nevertheless, Sarlo mistakenly counts the inescapability of mediation or knowledge "outside of experience" as a reason for us to abandon the "very idea of truth" (163). Since there is no unmediated position from which we can see unmediated truth, we are left only with multiple truths. Once we surrender the possibility of the "truth" of the past, even though it is inevitably mediated, we are left with descriptions of how our knowledge is mediated—by language, by genre, and ultimately, by who we are, which brings us back to identity. To give up on truth because truth is mediated is to claim that the subject is just one of the many things that are relevant to the question of what is true, putting Sarlo back in line with the very "truth of the subject" that she sets out to critique (58). Thus, it could be said that Sarlo offers us a high-theory version of Beverley's subalternism, and that the difference between them is the difference between two ways of doing identity.

Rather than champion the idea that individual memory was a valuable tool for knowing about the past, much Latin Americanist thought has thus declared that the past should not be known but remembered. Writers such as Eduardo Galeano have complained that the past had been relegated to history, to something merely known. Instead, Galeano has argued, the past—even the past never experienced by anyone living today—should be remembered.

In the preface to *Genesis* (1982), the first book in the trilogy that makes up *Memory of Fire* (1982–1986), Galeano complains that history has "stopped breathing" and has been "buried [. . .] beneath statuary bronze and monumental marble."[49] *Memory of Fire* was written in the wake of Uruguay's military dictatorship, and one of its stated motives is the author's desire to "rescue" and correct "official Latin American history," which had been "kidnapped" and reduced to "a military parade of bigwigs" (xv). But *Memory of Fire* goes beyond the desire to know the past more fully, completely, or correctly. In fact, Galeano is not invested in knowing the past at all. He is invested in imagining a way to experience the past; Galeano wants to "talk" to the Latin American past and "ask her of what difficult clays she was born, from what acts of love and violation she comes" (xv). Despite the fact that Galeano calls his book a "historical narrative" made up of "historical episodes" that actually "happened" (xv), *Memory of Fire* rejects the past as an object of knowledge. Instead, even though *Genesis* deals with events "from the end of the fifteenth century to the year 1700" (xvi), Galeano wants to turn those events into "memory" (xv).

Whereas Galeano wants Latin Americans to remember a history that never happened to them, Gustavo Verdesio wants Uruguayans to understand their unknown past as having been forgotten. In "An Amnesiac Nation: The Erasure of Indigenous Pasts by Uruguayan Expert Knowledges" (2003), Verdesio criticizes the widespread and systematic "lack of interest in both the colonial past and the indigenous history" of Uruguay.[50] Verdesio refers to the nineteenth-century "genocide of the Charrúa people" (202), which emerged from Uruguay's confrontation with "the problem of not being a nation in the same sense that the European ones were" and the resulting attempts to generate a homogeneous "national history" and "national culture" (197). The massacre of Charrúa people by Uruguay's first national government in 1831 was followed, Verdesio points out, by the institutional failure to recognize "the possible indigenous [. . .] contributions to [the] historical evolution" of Uruguay, a country "always imagined" by the Creole establishment as "a European nation" (202). Verdesio notes that "if a foreign observer desired to write a history of the cultural and social evolution in the territory of present-day Uruguay, he or she would conclude that, according to the available bibliography, the colonial past and the pre-Columbian era were almost nonexistent" or that "their importance was almost nil" (205). Of the "very few academic works about the pre-Columbian era in the territory," most, Verdesio argues, either rely too closely on chroniclers of the colonial period of dubious veracity (who reproduce and historically validate the myth of Charrúa barbarism and cannibalism) or "locate the Amerindians [of Uruguay] in a universal continuum" that places them "in a stage of evolution previous to the one reached by modern-day Western civilization" (207). Hence it is time, argues Verdesio, for a new and "rigorous study of [. . .] documentary sources and the most recent archaeological excavations" to "approach the indigenous past in a way that is less uncertain" (224). In this sense, Verdesio's project calls for historical revisionism and revised historical knowledge.

But it is not enough for Verdesio that Uruguayans simply revise the history of the territory that is "present-day Uruguay" so as to include a heightened recognition of its pre-Columbian history, or that these revisions provide an account of Amerindians outside the ideology of "national narratives," or that some speak out "to condemn the genocide" of the Charrúa (202), or even that new accounts of the Charrúa repudiate the "evolutionary model" (213) that subordinates them to supposedly more "advanced" Amerindian and non-Amerindian cultures. For Verdesio, only a change in the status of the Amerindian past will suffice. Verdesio does not want Uruguayans to *learn* the pre-Columbian and colonial history of the Amerindians; rather, he wants them to *remember* it, or at a minimum, to understand themselves as having forgotten it.

Verdesio wants the Amerindians to be remembered not in spite of but especially because of his own admissions about the lack of survival of Amerindian cultures in Uruguay. Not only did the "Amerindians from Uruguay [. . .] not leave many traces of their life on earth" (211) but also, he points out, despite the presence of some "individuals with indigenous biological heritage," indigenous culture "did not exist as such in Uruguay" after the 1870s (203). But if the culture of the Amerindians has "disappeared," and if their history has been "suppressed" since at least the 1870s, how can the present-day Uruguayans be expected to remember it, especially given that the basis for Verdesio's argument is that present-day Uruguayans never experienced it to begin with?

Although it seems impossible to imagine how we can remember things that we have never experienced, what is required by Galeano and Verdesio is the redescription of certain events of the past, given who we are. It is precisely because of this fact, and not in spite of it, that such projects do their work, since we have to figure out who we are *before* we can know which of the events in the past that we never experienced to call memory and which to call history. Everyone learns about the Charrúa past the same way, but only Uruguayans can (and should) think of themselves as remembering it. In this way, the indigenous Charrúa past becomes a marker of identitarian difference, but without the burdens of having to be culturally Charrúa.

Jean Franco is critical of Galeano's *Memory of Fire* because the sources that Galeano uses to "rescue" memory turn out to be only "texts" and not "oral tradition," "performances," or "myths."[51] Oral tradition, she writes, has "a special relation to memory."[52] But even if one believes that orality or cultural performance offers us better, more accurate, or more politically valuable accounts of the past than archives or texts, it would seem that they still count as representations through which viewers or listeners learn about the past and know it rather than remember it. Events in the past that we learn about through orality or performance, then, are no more part of our memory than events that we read about.

The common objection to this might be that memories are "cultural" or "collective," and that the split between experience and knowledge does not hold. For example, there is the idea, derived from the work of Maurice Halbwachs, of "historical memory" that "refers to residues of events by virtue of which groups claim a continuous identity through time."[53] Following this line of argument, having a historical memory of "the U.S. Civil War, for instance, is part of what it means to be an American and is part of the collective narrative of the United States," even if no one has an individual memory of the event.[54] But it cannot be having a "historical memory" of the Civil War that makes people Americans; it is because people first identify themselves as Americans that they know to think that the Civil War is part of their memory. Americans who think that the Civil War counts as part of their memory learn about it in the same ways that people all over the world learn about it: through linguistic or visual representations (such as history books, monuments, documentaries, or storytelling) and *not* through their experience of the actual event. There is no epistemological difference between the way present-day Americans access the Civil War and the way people all around the world do. It is only a claim of identity ("I am an American") that renames knowledge as memory, but that is to realize that the Civil War is not a memory at all. The same would be true, for example, if we were to claim that something in the past narrated to us by our grandparents counted as part of our memory: it is only because we first make a claim of identity between ourselves and our grandparents that we can then rename their narrative as our memory. The content of their narrative is not intrinsically any more a memory for us than for a total stranger: it does not come to us as an experience that we remember. We can begin to think of it as a memory only after we have claimed a shared identity with our grandparents. Thus, the claim of historical or cultural memory does not challenge the difference between knowledge and experience, and it does not make sense of someone thinking of something they never experienced.

In *The Archive and the Repertoire: Performing Cultural Difference in the Americas* (2003), Diana Taylor also seeks ways for the past to count as the experience and identity of people in the present. To that end, Taylor argues that performances function as "vital acts of transfer, transmitting social knowledge, memory, and a sense of identity" (2). Central to Taylor's argument is the idea that after the conquest, writing gained legitimization over "other totemic and mnemonic systems" at the same time that "indigenous and marginal populations of the colonial period" were denied "access to systematic writing" (18). Since those "who controlled writing, first the friars, then the *letrados* [, . . .] gained an inordinate amount of power," nonverbal practices "such as dance [. . .] and cooking," which had "long served to preserve a sense of communal identity and memory, were not considered valid forms of knowledge" (18). The "archive" was constructed to include only "documents, maps, literary texts, letters," which were bound up with the history of power, and not performances, which were "thought of as ephemeral, nonreproducible knowledge" (20). To correct this, Taylor proposes the idea of the "repertoire," a kind of performance equivalent of the archive that "allows scholars to trace traditions and influences" (20).

Even if we understand performance as constituting an archive or "repertoire," it is hard to see how or why things we find in an archive— even a performative one—can constitute memory instead of knowledge. But, Taylor argues, the "repertoire" turns events in the past into memory because first, the "repertoire [. . .] enacts embodied memory," and second, it requires "presence: people participate [. . .] by 'being there,' being part of the transmission" (20). Taylor quotes J. L. Austin's speech act theory, which claims that "the issuing of an utterance is the performing of an action."[55] Since the viewer participates in a performance, as Taylor argues, by "being there," we can supposedly move from thinking of ourselves as learning about something in the past to thinking that traditions are "transmitted 'live' in the here and now" and thus "experienced as present" (24). Whereas the viewer of the performance gets to count these "transmissions" as "experience," the performer gets to actually *embody* the past since, Taylor argues, "traditions are stored in the body" (24). The idea is that viewers experience the transmission of "traditions" through a performance, then can re-perform them. By re-performing these traditions, we can think not only that we remember things but also that we embody them.

The appeal of Taylor's account of performance is that it establishes performance as "an important system of knowing and transmitting knowledge" that, unlike a text, has "no claims on meaning" (25). Indeed, performance is imagined as a way to sidestep the autonomy of meaning from the reading subject in texts. Hence Taylor argues that performance refuses the "unidirectionality of meaning making" (8). If meaning in performance is multidirectional, then Taylor's viewers can all at once experience a "transmitted" past, embody the past by performing the "traditions" they have viewed, and look at the performed past and see themselves, since what they are looking at, multidirectionally, must be at least in part the result of who they are.

The dominant trend in the Latin American novel since the late 1970s, as Seymour Menton suggests, has been the proliferation of what he calls "New Historical Novels."[56] These "new" historical novels, Menton states, are just as historical as the old ones—inasmuch as they are about the historical past—but they differ in that they are less concerned with producing a "more or less faithful re-creation, albeit artistically embellished," of the past (19). Instead, argues Menton, the new historical novel in Latin America is characterized by a "set of [. . .] traits" (22) that includes the "subordination [. . .] of the mimetic re-creation of a given historical period to [. . .] philosophical ideas," such as the idea of "the impossibility of ascertaining the true nature of reality or history" (23).

In similar fashion, Raymond L. Williams argues that the primary concern of what he calls the Latin American "postmodern novel" is "truth," by which he means "truths [that] are fundamentally contextual"; in place of "universally valid truths," in these novels there emerges "a generalized mistrust of the capacity of any language to render truths about the world."[57] In Juan José Saer's *The Witness* (1983), for example, the narrator sets out to tell the story of his life among a group of Indians known as the Colastiné. But in the end, as Rolena Adorno has correctly observed, "his attempts at writing about them only reveal himself."[58] But if this realization counts as a defeat for those who want to know the past, it is a victory for those who, like Bonfil, want to think of the historical past as alive in the present and thus somehow part of our identity.[59] It is no surprise, then, that many Latin American novels in the 1980s and 1990s were preoccupied with, on the one hand, the project of re-narrating the historical past and, on the other hand, the idea that, as Keith Jenkins puts it, the "past that we 'know' is always contingent upon our own views, our own 'present.'"[60] If we think that history is "inevitably a personal construct, a manifestation of the historian's perspective as a 'narrator,'" then we can think that by looking at the past we can see ourselves.[61]

One of the narrators in Carmen Boullosa's *Cielos de la tierra* (1997) lives in a "Colony of Survivors" called L'Atlàntide, a place "suspended" in the Earth's atmosphere roughly 213 years after the Earth has been rendered uninhabitable as the result of nuclear war.[62] In L'Atlàntide, "everything is air"—the houses are made of air, clothes are made of air, and people are "invisible and incorporeal" (17). The novel's narrator, Lear, lives on L'Atlàntide and declares that "this is the Air Age," and in the "Air Age," she explains, air has been domesticated (17). This means that there are no "hurricanes" or "tornadoes," no hot or cold (17). Despite the fact that in L'Atlàntide there is no poverty, disease, old age, or even death, Lear seems preoccupied with the question of "surviving" (20). Since Lear firmly believes that "remembering is surviving," she does have a reason to be worried about "surviving" (20). In L'Atlàntide, Lear states, the inhabitants believe that they should only "concern themselves with the present and the future" and "forget the past" (18)—a politics that the novel sees as a kind of repetition of colonialism, the Mexican Revolution, the Cuban Revolution, and the Boom.

Thus, in spite of the fact that the official policy on L'Atlàntide is that the "past" should be "erased" (18), Lear is obsessed with the past, which in L'Atlàntide has come to be known as the "time of History" (15) on planet Earth, now in ruins and uninhabited. Lear is, in fact, so obsessed with the past that she has made it her vocation: "I do archaeology," she says, "and I am the only one who does this in my community" (15). Despite Lear's repeated insistence that in L'Atlàntide the past has been forgotten or erased, she admits that the "works of art which deserved a space on Earth" are on display in L'Atlàntide in "a museum which we named Das Menschen Museum, the Museum of Man," but she complains that "no one visits it" (21). Lear also admits that the authorities of L'Atlàntide have preserved two thousand texts from the "time of History," a list that includes Newton's *Principia Mathematica*, Goethe's *Theory of Colors*, and Stowe's *Uncle Tom's Cabin*. Even the Earth itself, albeit in ruins, has been preserved: "we left all their trash on the Earth," Lear notes; "we reconstructed all the gardens, but left all the trash and rubble intact" (20). The inhabitants of L'Atlàntide have built a stairway of "solid air" called Punto Calpe that "joins L'Atlàntide with Earth" (24)—a stairway that Lear uses to do fruitful research in the ruins of the John Carter Brown Library, the British Library, and other national libraries and archives, in "Madrid, Bogotá, Paris, Mexico City" (22). All the material once held in the Library of Congress in Washington, Lear notes, was put onto microfilm at the outbreak of the "intercontinental war" that destroyed life on Earth (14). Lear's concerns about the past being erased on L'Atlàntide therefore seem puzzling, given her own admissions regarding the abundance of what she calls "objects" from or about the past, and especially given the institutionalized preservation of these objects by the authorities on L'Atlàntide (21). It would seem that anyone living on L'Atlàntide interested in learning about the past could easily do so given the breadth and depth of material from and about that past. But for Lear, this is precisely the problem, and this is the ground for her disagreement with the authorities of L'Atlàntide.

For the authorities, the past is something that is learned about; for Lear, the past is something that should be remembered. The authorities of L'Atlàntide see their relationship to the past as essentially about knowledge, whereas Lear wants her relationship with the past to be essentially about identity. It is this difference between the past as an object of study and as a source of experience and identity that Lear, and the novel as a whole, seeks to undo. Lear complains that "nobody in L'Atlàntide wants to recognize their forefathers in the men of History, much less find their origins in them" (15). She declares that "with my studies I want to return to our forefathers, I want to reconstruct them," and she explains that she turned to the study of history because "I don't know who my father was or who my mother was because I was conceived in a reproduction machine" (15). Even though Lear does not have biological parents, her study of history is the search for biological parents—for the kind of relationship with the past constituted by biology. In fact, Lear states that one of the main problems with the inhabitants of L'Atlàntide is that they do not think of themselves as descendants of anyone at all: they "are what they wanted to be, children of themselves" (306). Without a biological mother or father, Lear complains precisely about not being able to appeal to the biological logic that "men in the time of History used to figure out who I am" (15); thus she expects the past to do the work that neither culture nor biology (Lear does not even have a body) can do. In the novel, Lear's culture is radically discontinuous with past cultures, and she has only a bric-a-brac assortment of cultural artifacts, without any sense of which ones are properly hers.

Although Lear professes to be an "archaeologist" obsessed with the past, she declares that "objects" hold no interest for her (21). Books—more specifically autobiography and historical narrative—have become her only source of interest, and indeed, they come to offer her the kind of relationship to the past that she desires. This is because of, and not in spite of, the fact that Boullosa's novel, like much of what Linda Hutcheon has called "historiographic metafiction," problematizes the idea of historical knowledge and "blur[s] the line between fiction and history."[63] Postmodern historiography, Hutcheon argues, reorients the question posed to historical discourse from "'to what empirically real object in the past does the language of history refer?'" toward "'to which discursive context could this language belong?'"[64] This poses a problem if we want to know the past, but it poses no problem whatsoever if we want to make history ours and use it to give us an identity. The fulfillment of Lear's identity through history involves, not surprisingly, taking up the act of narration. Specifically, Lear translates and re-narrates a manuscript she has found among the ruins on planet Earth, a translation of a book written in Latin by Hernando de Rivas, a Nahuatl, about colonial life after the fall of Tenochtitlan (1521–1590). Rivas's book was found in the 1990s by Estela Díaz, one of the narrators in the novel, who decides to translate it into Spanish even though she claims that it should really be translated into Nahuatl. Estela is unhappy because the radical politics she practiced during the sixties and seventies "erased [. . .] our colonial past," so she decides to translate "an Indian's text" (204). By translating it, by the mere act of representing history that then allows her to see herself in her own representation, Estela discovers that the manuscript "belongs to me, speaks to me from the sixteenth century, explains my present" (67).

Boullosa insists that her novel is not a novel "by an author, but by authors" (9). As she translates Hernando de Rivas's manuscript in the 1990s, Estela begins to talk about her own life; upon realizing that she has ended up telling her whole life story, from childhood to the present, she asks herself, "Why did I begin my story that way?" (163). The novel's insistent answer is that this is how Rivas told the story of his own life: Rivas writes in Latin that "I want to tell my life story from beginning to end, and for that reason I will begin with where, when, and how I was born" (79). Thus, the kind of identity Estela could not have with indigenous people like Rivas in culture, because "our [. . .] past" was erased, is achieved through narrative; Estela becomes part of Rivas by "lying here and there" (205) as she translates his story, and Rivas becomes part of Estela once she finds herself only speaking and writing within the discursive conventions and parameters she inherits from him. This realization is what Hutcheon characterizes as the moment when we supposedly realize that in making the past "rewritten" we make it "re-lived"; and this is also the realization that forms the basis for the technology in the novel that makes it possible for Lear to see herself and find herself in a past that she never lived in.[65] Since writing history involves writing it from our own point of view, it becomes possible to look at our account of the past and see ourselves—and think that the difference located there is our own.

It is tempting to think that the main problem with memory is that it invokes the identitarian difference of people in the past to constitute the identitarian difference of people in the present. It is also tempting to think of a solution in terms of a resuscitated Latin American culturalist project in which identitarian difference would be imagined once again in terms of culture rather than in terms of history and memory. The problem with memory, however, is not that it commits us to an inefficacious version of identity, but that it commits us to identity in the first place. The political stakes and continuity of that commitment can be seen in Jean Franco's *Cruel Modernity* (2013), in which violence and atrocity in the recent past is understood as the reenactment of violence and atrocity in the distant past.

In relation to her discussion of a 2004 video filmed in Nicaragua by the North American photographer Susan Meiselas, Franco writes that Meiselas's video not only reveals how "the present remembers or relives the past," but also shows "how mobile history is, how it is constantly reiterated and reformulated."[66] To be sure, the idea that the present is a reliving of the past is central to *Cruel Modernity*, and it is the basis for Franco's argument that the history of violence and atrocity in the recent Latin American past should be understood as a reenactment of the Spanish conquest of the Americas. The conquest, for Franco, was the moment that reified racial and gender hierarchies and set into motion "a modern project that drags on a colonial inheritance" (63). Thus, she argues, "the myths and prejudices inherited from the conquest [. . .] came to support the intellectual arguments that upheld the military project in Guatemala and the neoliberal project in Peru" (47). For example, Franco notes that "the special forces of the Guatemalan army appropriated the name *kaibiles* from an Indian chief who fought against the conqueror Pedro de Alvarado," and they did so "as if the conquest were still going on" (5–6). Violence in the "present-day," Franco suggests, is linked to "the Spanish army and the wars of independence" and is "a reenactment of the conquest itself" that seeks to "finish the work of the conquest" (79).

Franco argues that "over the centuries, the alibi for the subjugation of the indigenous was constantly reformulated according to the needs of the state and the definition of nationhood and in hundreds of different scenarios" (46). In other words, Franco suggests that the different politics and ideologies involved in the subjugation of the indigenous were merely alibis, which is to say, excuses or rationalizations that covered over a supposedly real motive that cannot be fully "rationalized or explained" (49). That supposedly real motive, Franco suggests, is a persistent racism or "contempt" for indigenous people that has its origins in Latin America's colonial period (57). The result of seeing conflicts such as the civil war in Guatemala as simply one of many manifestations of a persistent "conscious or unconscious racism" (49) or "hatred of the indigenous" (54) makes an entire history of violence and atrocity comprehensible only as the byproduct of attitudes toward identitarian difference. Moreover, the idea that "myths and prejudices inherited from the conquest" are behind violence and atrocity radically ontologizes both the actions of the victimizers and the experiences of the victims. Hardly anyone would doubt the claim that racism exists today throughout the Americas, or that it is a phenomenon that negatively affects many millions of people on a daily basis. Likewise, hardly anyone would doubt the fact that racism primarily explains why, as Franco suggests, "at some moments during [Guatemala's] civil war, the number of Maya victims was higher and why extreme acts of cruelty took place in their communities" (49). Nevertheless, what is at issue is the difference between the question of why some people were more victimized than others and the question of why there were any victims at all. The idea that acts of violence reenact the conquest provides an answer to only the former. Consider, for example, Franco's discussion of Peru's civil war: she quotes the president of Peru's Truth and Reconciliation Commission, who claimed that "two decades of destruction and death would not have been possible without the profound contempt towards the dispossessed people of the country, expressed equally by members of the insurgent Sendero Luminoso (Shining Path) and the Army, a contempt that is woven into every moment of Peruvian everyday life" (56). It might well be the case that both the Sendero Luminoso and the Peruvian army equally shared "contempt" for "dispossessed people." However, to think that the civil war is explained by "contempt" entails committing to a politics in which contempt's antonym—respect—is the basis for an affective politics. In other words, we might ask ourselves whether this way of understanding violence reduces all conflicts in Latin American history to conflicts between identities or between two competing attitudes toward "ethnic difference"—it is either respected or despised. Celebrating it is obviously the right choice, but we should ask ourselves who benefits at whose expense when politics is reduced to that choice—when, in other words, the Sendero Luminoso and the Peruvian army are thought to be merely two different faces of sadism, or when respect for the poor, rather than ending poverty, becomes the cornerstone of politics for the Left.

A New Latin Americanism?

JOHN BEVERLEY'S *LATINAMERICANISM AFTER 9/11* (2011) is an attempt to revise Latin Americanist literary, cultural, and political theory for the twenty-first century. Released almost exactly ten years after the events of September 11, 2001, it reconsiders the preceding decade in terms of both Latin America and Latin Americanism. If 9/11 marked what Beverley describes as a geopolitical sea change, then, he argues, it also marked a disciplinary one. After all, in September 2001, only days before the attacks on the World Trade Center and the Pentagon, "the disbanding of the Latin American Subaltern Studies Group was announced publicly" at the Latin American Studies Association conference in Washington, D.C.[1] At the same time that the world changed, so too did the field, only not enough, Beverley insists, to address the vast and complex aftermath of 9/11. Thus Beverley's book is, on the one hand, about what he identifies as a "shift away from identification with U.S. power post-9/11" (6) and, on the other, about the possibility of a new Latin Americanism that might properly account for, and make a difference to, "politics on the ground" throughout the region (9).

Beverley rightly identifies a crisis of disciplinary and theoretical practice in the field. However, the solution he proposes involves not a *new* Latin Americanism but rather a retrenchment into the same "ossified discourses and expectations" that he seeks to repudiate (15). *Latinamericanism after 9/11* gives urgency to the task of rethinking the assumptions and ideologies embedded in Latin Americanism, inasmuch as Beverley is breathing new life into them.

In confronting the changes in both the world and the field over the past ten years, Beverley finds that Latin Americanist discourses—such as subaltern studies, deconstruction, and neo-Arielism—have reached a limit of some form or another. Dominant forms of Latin Americanism, says Beverley, are either irrelevant, exhausted, out of touch with "politics on the ground" (9), or still bound up in "the tradition of the Latin American 'lettered city'" (23). For example, he declares that *Latinamericanism after 9/11* is a "postsubalternist" book (8). The investment in "the separation of the state and the subaltern" on the part of subaltern studies must be rethought, he suggests, given that in "the case of several governments of the marea rosada, social movements from the popular-subaltern sectors of society have 'become the state'" (9). Likewise, he argues, "deconstruction is yielding diminishing and politically ambiguous returns, and [. . .] this has something to do with the way in which both 9/11 and the emergence of the marea rosada have shifted the grounds of theory and criticism in our time" (9). Neo-Arielism, Beverley suggests, is "antineoliberal," but he sees it as problematic because it is "suspicious of the new forms of agency emerging from the social movements and corresponding new forms of radical or 'populist' politics" (22).

Beverley identifies the main problem facing the field: "if we still accept the principles of cultural democratization and egalitarianism as a goal, today we find ourselves in a situation in which what we do can be complicit with precisely that which we want to resist: the deconstructive force of the market and neoliberal ideology" (21). Therefore, "the task that faces the Latinamericanist project today has to begin with the recognition that globalization and neoliberal political economy have done, more effectively than ourselves, the work of cultural democratization and dehierarchization" (21). Moreover, he writes, "neoliberalism—in spite of its origins in extreme counterrevolutionary violence—became an ideology in which some sectors of subaltern classes or groups could also see possibilities for themselves" (21).

To be sure, the last thirty years of neoliberal economic policies in Latin America have coincided with unprecedented identitarian recognition and cultural dehierarchization. As Donna Lee Van Cott points out, in the 1990s "most Latin American countries underwent significant constitutional reforms," and almost all "of the new constitutions incorporated language that formally recognized the identities and rights of their populations for the first time."[2] Bolivia's 1994 constitution, for example, defined the nation as "free, independent, sovereign, multiethnic and pluricultural."[3] Peru's 1993 constitution declared that the "State recognizes and protects the ethnic and cultural plurality of the Nation," and Colombia's 1991 constitution protected "the ethnic and cultural diversity of the Colombian Nation."[4] Moreover, the new constitutions of Colombia, Ecuador, and Peru all made indigenous languages official in indigenous territories.[5]

Although these reforms marked a triumph for *cultural* equality, they went hand in hand with a series of reforms that have been a defeat for *economic* equality. The same Mexican constitution of 1994 that recognized the "pluricultural" character of Mexico also dismantled, under pressure from the World Bank, Mexican revolutionary agrarian reform. Likewise, the Peruvian constitution of 1993, which both declared that all Peruvians have a right to their own "ethnic and cultural identity" and affirmed the state's respect for "the cultural identity of the rural and native communities," also opened up the sale of communal lands.[6] As Xavier Albó points out, not all the changes in Peru's 1993 constitution were "the result of pressures from below."[7] "There are clearly international factors," argues Albó, that simultaneously emphasize "the importance of multiethnicity" and also "insist on the need for open markets."[8] In the plainest terms, for at least the last twenty years in Latin America, cultural identities have been winning, while poor people have been losing. In Mexico alone, the neoliberal restructuring that took place in the 1980s and 1990s produced 24 billionaires, a majority of whom participated in the privatizations carried out during the Salinas presidency.[9] In 1996 the richest 10 percent of Mexican households controlled 36.6 percent of the wealth; in 2008 these same households controlled 41.4 percent of the wealth.[10] But more dramatic than internal economic inequalities are global ones: Latin American per capita income, when it is rendered as a percentage of U.S. per capita income, has been steadily declining for decades. In 1950 Latin American per capita income was roughly 45 percent of the per capita income in the United States; by 1985 that number had dropped to almost 35 percent, and in 2001 it was 25 percent.[11]

In a world characterized by greater cultural recognition and increasing economic equality, Beverley surprisingly declares that the "possibility of fashioning a new Latin Americanism" involves "recovering for the discourse of the Left the space of cultural dehierarchization ceded to the market and to neoliberalism" (23). But if cultural dehierarchization is now hegemonic, it is hard to see why it should be recovered as a discourse for the Left—or for anyone. The short answer is that realizing that the neoliberal market has brought about what Beverley calls "a play of differences that is not subject, in principle, to the dialectic of the master and the slave" (22) amounts to a *game over* on two counts for Latin Americanism. First, inasmuch as Latin Americanism involves cultural dehierarchization, then the recognition of cultural dehierarchization's hegemony leaves it without anything to do. Second, the fact that cultural dehierarchization was achieved by and in neoliberalism poses the question of whether that project was or is now a progressive and efficacious form of resistance to capitalism.

Beverley's *Latinamericanism after 9/11* is in many ways an important account of the political exhaustion of Latin Americanist ideologies—especially given their apparent complicity with the logic of neoliberalism. For example, Beverley insists, as he has before, that a new Latin Americanism "cannot come principally from the economic and cultural elites" and instead must come from "a cultural intentionality that arises from 'others'" (23). But if for Beverley Latin America has suffered from "the excessive presence of the intellectual class" and the imposition of "its own values and ambitions in the formulation of models of identity, governability, and development" (22), now he must recognize that "globalization entails a displacement of the authority of Latin American intellectuals" (66). "Neoliberal policies," he notes, have been what has displaced the Latin American intellectual, because these policies "have restructured the Latin American university and secondary education system, and revalorized what counts as significant academic or professional credentials in a way that devalued literary or humanistic knowledge" (67). In other words, Beverley writes, the "dehierarchization implicit in neoliberal theory and policy also entails [. . .] a strong challenge to the authority of intellectual elites in determining standards of cultural value" (73).

The "main point of convergence" between subaltern studies and cultural studies, writes Beverley, was "a sense that cultural democratization implies a shift of hermeneutic authority from the philological-critical activity of the 'lettered city' to popular reception, a shift that entails a corresponding displacement of the authority of what Gramsci called the traditional intellectual" (67). However, Beverley notes, "neoliberal theory" has set aside "the values of both traditional and modern intellectuals" (22), and he is right to suggest that "neoliberalism does not propose any a priori hierarchy of value other than the existence of consumer desire as such" (73). Neoliberal technocrats and markets, not Latin Americanist projects, put the nail in the coffin of the "lettered city" and carried out the task of "relativizing the authority of academic knowledge" once assigned to *testimonio* and the subaltern.[12] What is left for Latin Americanism, then? By way of an answer, Beverley enthusiastically endorses the political potential of groups such as Comuna, an academic collective in Bolivia that "resembled in some ways both the South Asian and the Latin American Subaltern Studies Groups"

(10). Álvaro García Linera, the current vice president of Bolivia, was associated with the group in the 1990s and "probably read" an anthology of essays, edited by Bolivian academics close to the group, that included Spivak's "Deconstructing Historiography" (10). The lesson to be learned here, then, is that "theory can have consequences" that "can be enabling for political practice" (10), bringing the intellectual elite back into the political picture in a striking way.

In the face of the victories of Latin Americanist cultural politics within neoliberal hegemony, Beverley sets out to identify what might be "the form of a *new* Latinamericanism, capable of confronting U.S. hegemony and expressing an alternative future for the peoples of the Americas" (18). But Beverley's *new* Latin Americanism sounds almost like a definition of the *old* one. Take, for example, Beverley's description of the new Latin Americanist project he is proposing, which will center around "the affirmation of the distinctness of Latin America as a 'civilization' in the face of North American and European domination, without falling back on the exhausted formulas of a complacent creole-mestizo nationalism" (23). Besides the reference to the "exhausted formulas" of "creole-mestizo nationalism," this could be a gloss of any number of classic Latin Americanist texts such as, for example, Rubén Darío's "A Roosevelt" (1904). But then "creole-mestizo nationalism" itself reemerges in Beverley's project when he declares that what is needed is "the survival and demographic recovery of the indigenous peoples of the continent with their own languages, cultures, and economies, not just as semiautonomous groups within existing nation-states, but rather as constitutive elements of the identity of those nations and of Latin America itself" (24). What is that if not a version of creole-mestizo nationalism? The desire to recover and integrate racial others "as constitutive elements of the identity of [. . .] nations" drives not only José Martí's "Nuestra América" but also any number of canonical Latin Americanist projects, such as Manuel Gamio's *indigenismo*, Nicolás Guillén's *afrocubanismo*, or José Carlos Mariátegui's indigenous socialism, just to name a few. In subaltern studies there was at least a certain skepticism about the state that created a distance between subaltern studies and Latin American nationalisms. However, now that "popular-subaltern sectors of society have 'become the state'" (9), previously suppressed nationalist thinking can reemerge in service of a "popular-subaltern" politics.[13]

In Latin Americanism, the main criteria for political ideologies have often centered on the question of whether a given ideology is legitimately ours—what Augusto Salazar Bondy once called a "filosofía propia."[14] Beverley declares in his introduction that there is "no clear line of separation" between "identity politics [. . .] and politics" (5). Indeed, politics in *Latinamericanism after 9/11* crucially involves recovering and recognizing identities and subject positions buried beneath layers of imported practices and beliefs—what Beverley calls "the emancipation of Latin America *as Latin America*" (25). The echo of classic Latin Americanism could not be more clearly heard here. Beverley's project recalls, for example, Martí's idea that the "form of the government must be in harmony with the country's natural constitution" (290), which first requires that that "natural constitution" be made manifest in the authentic cultural expression of the *pueblo*—that is, in Beverley's words, the "ways of thinking and being that have been suppressed [. . .] for centuries" (58–59). This explains, then, the grounds for Beverley's enthusiasm for the *marea rosada*: it constitutes a "Latin Americanism articulated 'from' the subaltern" (23) and springs from "the theoretical originality produced by the Latin American social movements, which have been not only 'objects' of theory but also its creators" (24).

Latinamericanism after 9/11 is also interested in "displacing" capitalism (23) and finding ways for workers to confront "increasingly brutal capitalist regimes, to take control of the forces of production [. . .] in their own name as a class" (24). Curiously, however, Beverley insists that "probably the vast majority" of Bolivians imagine "social justice" not in terms of national or global economic redistribution but instead as "a recognition by and *in* the state" of suppressed "languages and ways of thinking" (59). Not only are these two projects *not* related, but they also exist in tension with each other. Consider, for example, what Nancy Fraser calls the "redistribution-recognition dilemma."[15] According to Fraser, "the politics of recognition and the politics of redistribution often appear to have mutually contradictory aims. Whereas the first tends to promote group differentiation, the second tends to undermine it. Thus, the two kinds of claim stand in tension with each other; they can interfere with, or even work against, each other" (16). The tension between recognition, which seeks to solve the problem of cultural injustice, and redistribution, which seeks to solve the problem of economic injustice, lies in two "correspondingly distinct kinds of remedy" (15). In economic injustice, the problem is that a certain group "receives an unjustly large share of the burdens and an unjustly small share of the rewards" (17). Because class is essentially "a mode of social differentiation that is rooted in the political-economic structure of society," the remedy for class exploitation is "redistribution, not recognition" (17). Ultimately, although that task will involve the proletariat identifying itself as a distinct collective, the "last thing it needs is recognition of its difference" (18). Instead, the goal will be "abolishing the class structure as such" and putting "the proletariat out of business as a group" (17–18). The remedy for cultural injustice, however, "will be cultural recognition, as opposed to political-economic redistribution" (18).

Whereas Fraser seeks to find a way to reconcile "the politics of redistribution and the politics of recognition" (23), Walter Benn Michaels argues that recognition demands undermine redistribution demands by giving us "a vision of difference without inequality."[16] Recognition, then, "gives us a model of differences we can love, like those between Asian Americans and Caucasians," rather than differences between "rich people and poor people" that are less appealing (84). Take, for example, Fraser's claim that race is "a bivalent mode of collectivity with both a political-economic face and a cultural-valuational face" (22); redressing racial injustice therefore "requires changing both political economy and culture" (22).

Michaels, however, has shown that fixing racial (or generally identitarian) inequality poses no inherent challenge to the economic status quo. In other words, racial equality in the United States is commonly understood to mean erasing the "economic gap" between whites and blacks, rather than erasing the gap between rich and poor. When racial equality is the problem to be overcome, the solution involves merely making sure that blacks are

> proportionally represented (13 percent) at every level of American society. Where, in other words, blacks currently make up a disproportionately large segment (around 20 percent) of the population with a household income under $15,000, they would, if we could [repair racial inequality], make up only 13 percent. And where they now account for only about 7 percent of the households earning above $75,000, they would [. . .] make up 13 percent of that group, too. This wouldn't, of course, eliminate economic inequality. But while the gap between the rich and the poor would remain, the gap between black and white would disappear; inequality would no longer be racialized.[17]

This enables the liberal fantasy of creating equal opportunity or an even playing field. The result is that once these goals are achieved, the economic inequality that remains is no longer "unjust"; inequality and poverty become acceptable as long as they are not the product of identitarian injustice. The project of achieving identitarian equality solves one inequality (identity) and leaves another one intact (economic); the struggle for economic equality solves both. Given that the last thirty years—in both Latin America and the United States—have witnessed a simultaneous growth of recognition *and* economic inequality, recognition politics should at the very least be regarded with suspicion. "Greater indifference to inequality," writes Michaels, "is happily accompanied by greater attachment to identity" (158). This is essentially what the commitment to cultural equality is about, "since a world of people who are different from us looks a lot more appealing than a world of people who are poorer than us" (158). Cultural dehierarchization, in other words, "redescribes the material difference between people (I have more, you have less, too bad for you) as cultural difference (I have mine, you have yours, it's all good)" (161). Therefore, "there's nothing about [. . .] identities that in itself counts as a resistance to globalization" or economic inequality (143). Even worse, cultural dehierarchization works hand in hand with the two because it encourages us to think that as long as cultures are preserved and protected, justice has been achieved.

In the case of Latin America, the politics of cultural dehierarchization has created a machine by which hierarchies are endlessly redescribed as difference, which in turn is celebrated as such. The result is a diminished political vocabulary for thinking about something that is necessarily hierarchical and identifying something in which difference is not valuable: namely, class. Solving the problem of economic injustice entails erasing difference, whereas the problem of cultural injustice entails celebrating and even preserving it. The objection to this is that *we can do both.* But the question remains as to how, within the seemingly centrifugal logic of difference as intrinsically valuable (or the powerful forces of neoliberalism Beverley identifies), we might be able to distinguish between, on the one hand, cultural differences that should be preserved and celebrated and, on the other hand, economic differences that should be eliminated.

Indeed, the work of anthropologists such as Carmen Martínez Novo has persuasively shown the difficulty of differentiating between what is part of a "cultural tradition" to be respected and what is the manifestation of an economic "necessity."[18] In her study of Mixtec migrant workers, Martínez Novo writes that as she was beginning her work, she expected to find both "a vibrant indigenous movement struggling for indigenous rights and against the exploitation of border employers" and the Mexican government "repress[ing] this movement on behalf of capitalists" (5–6). Instead, she found "government officials organizing and funding indigenous groups and insisting that migrants remain so identified" despite the fact that "many grassroots Mixtecs [. . .] were reluctant to pursue this agenda, because they preferred to melt in [. . .] and seek social mobility" (6). Moreover, Martínez Novo suggests, "much of what was identified and promoted as 'indigenous culture' by government-appointed and other advocates was either a stereotypical construction of 'Indianness' that had little to do with the actual experiences of Mixtec migrants or a manifestation of poverty that was naturalized as culture" (6). Martínez Novo discusses how, for example, some advocates on behalf of indigenous rights in Mexico have interpreted "street vending in the company of children as a choice or a cultural tradition instead of a necessity," even though indigenous women themselves "perceive child labor, including their own work when they were children, as an unfortunate consequence of economic need and not an ethnic custom" (110). Martínez Novo's point, in other words, is that "social inequality" is all too easily "naturalized when interpreted as culture" (110). Beverley, for example, conflates class with gender, race, ethnicity, and religious identity when he declares in *Subalternity and Representation* (1999) that "class is itself also an identity" (135). Should it then be preserved? Or understood in nonhierarchical terms? If not, what could function as the criteria by which certain aspects of "identity" are to be affirmed while others are erased?

The seemingly relentless ontologizing force in *Latinamericanism after 9/11* underscores the difficulty of establishing such criteria. Beverley unfortunately points to no way out, offering only a renewed commitment to identitarianism. Already in *Subalternity and Representation*, Beverley recognizes the limits of "distributing political energies along a line of proliferation of difference in an era of declining real incomes, structural unemployment, and downward social mobility" (153). And yet in that book, as in *Latinamericanism after 9/11*, he makes a strenuous effort to unite identitarianism, particularism, and egalitarianism.

Beverley is right to believe that Latin America has the potential to offer "an alternative future for the peoples of the Americas" (18). However, thinking of that alternative future in terms that are no longer identitarian might give Latin America's cultural and ideological alternatives new traction, and provide the necessary vocabulary for correcting the region's most grievous material injustices.

Notes

INTRODUCTION

1. Borges, "Conjectural Poem," 143. Further references are cited parenthetically in the text. Unless otherwise indicated in the bibliography, all translations from non-English-language texts are mine.

2. Sarmiento, *Facundo*, 35.

3. Mignolo, *Darker Side of Western Modernity*, xv–xvi.

4. Sarmiento, *Facundo*, 78.

5. See, for example, Boghossian, *Fear of Knowledge*, in which he discusses what he calls the "doctrine of equal validity" (3). "Especially within the academy, but also and inevitably to some extent outside of it," he argues, "the idea that there are 'many equally valid ways of knowing the world,' with science being just one of them, has taken very deep root" (2).

6. In *Exhaustion of Difference*, Moreiras explores the question of "Latin American Latin Americanists" who posit "location as final redemption" (6). The problem, writes Moreiras, is that "location was precisely what always already delegitimized their outsiding others" (6). Thus the question is, "How can location function simultaneously as a source of legitimation and its opposite?" (6). If the truth of what someone says depends on the subject position that person occupies, how can there be disagreements? See also Davidson, "Objectivity and Practical Reason." Davidson argues that "if people throw rocks or shout or shoot at each other, there is not necessarily, or perhaps even often, any proposition whose truth is in dispute" (21). A disagreement, he argues, "requires that there be some proposition, a shared content, about which opinions differ" (21). This, of course, runs counter to the account of disagreement famously offered by Jacques Rancière, for whom disagreement "is not the conflict between one who says white and another who says black" but rather the conflict "between one who says white and another who also says white but

does not understand the same thing by it or does not understand that the other is saying the same thing in the name of whiteness" (*Disagreement*, x).

7. Foley, for example, argues that "when I believe [something] and am aware that I believe it, I am pressured, given the nature of belief, to think that there is nothing amiss with my belief—it is true, reliably produced, justified, etc." (*When Is True Belief Knowledge?*, 101).

8. Balibar, "Racism as Universalism," 195.

9. In *Against Relativism*, Macklin critiques the fact that "there is often a tendency to defend the actions of marginalized groups even if those same actions would be condemned if carried out by the dominant or more powerful group" (7).

10. Laclau, "Structure, History and the Political," 209. Further references are cited parenthetically in the text.

11. Laclau, "Universalism, Particularism, and the Question of Identity," 90. Further references are cited parenthetically in the text.

12. Fish, "Reply," 925–926.

13. Ibid., 926.

14. Ibid., 927.

15. Fish, *Trouble with Principle*, 69.

16. Ibid., 70.

17. Haack, *Evidence and Inquiry*, 250.

18. The most important recent work on cosmopolitanism in Latin America includes Siskind, *Cosmopolitan Desires*; Loss, *Cosmopolitanisms and Latin America*; and Kozlarek, *Entre cosmopolitismo y "conciencia del mundo."*

19. Rama, *Lettered City*, 81.

20. Beverley, *Latinamericanism after 9/11*, 23. Further references are cited parenthetically in the text.

21. Acosta, *Thresholds of Illiteracy*, 3, 2.

22. Di Stefano and Sauri, "Making It Visible."

23. Ibid.

24. Moreiras, *Exhaustion of Difference*, 44.

25. Martí, *Selected Writings*, 296.

26. Balibar, "Is There a 'Neo-Racism'?," 24.

27. Fernández Retamar, *Caliban and Other Essays*, 95.

28. Ibid., 85.

29. Gamio, *Forjando patria*, 25; García Canclini, *Consumers and Citizens*, 114.

30. See, for example, Zea, *Pensamiento latinoamericano*; Roig, *Teoría y crítica*; and Cerutti Guldberg, *Filosofía de la liberación*. More recent works include Nuccetelli, *Latin American Thought*; Schutte, *Cultural Identity and Social Liberation*; and Larrain, *Identity and Modernity in Latin America*.

1. Martí, *Selected Writings*, 295. Further references are cited parenthetically in the text.

2. On the antiracist Cuban politics of Martí's "My Race," see Poey Baró, "'Race' and Anti-Racism."

3. Appiah defines racialism as the view "that there are heritable characteristics, possessed by members of our species, which allow us to divide them into a small set of races, in such a way that all the members of these races share certain traits and tendencies with each other that they do not share with members of any other race" (*In My Father's House*, 13). Moreover, Appiah suggests, "these traits and tendencies characteristic of a race constitute, on the racialist view, a sort of racial essence; it is part of the content of racialism that the essential heritable characteristics of the 'Races of Man' account for more than the visible morphological characteristics—skin color, hair type, facial features—on the basis of which we make our informal classifications" (13). For a similar definition of racialism, see Snyder, "Idea of Racialism."

4. Rodríguez-Luis, for example, describes the concept of *nuestra América* as "the cornerstone of Latin Americanism" ("Introduction," xvi). For a history of the concept of *nuestra América* in Latin American thought, see Almarza, "Frase 'nuestra América'"; and Sobrevilla, "Surgimiento de la idea."

5. Mignolo, "Afterword," 207; Coronil, *Magical State*, 13.

6. Saldívar, *Dialectics of Our America*, 4. Saldívar characterizes Martí as "a specific intellectual in Foucault's sense" and suggests that "Nuestra América" can provide "the central oppositional codes on which to base a dialectical view of the American continent and the Americas' many literatures" (7). Gillman makes a similar argument regarding the disciplinary potential and present-day relevance of "Nuestra América" when she writes that "José Martí has taken his place at the headwaters of a still uncompleted revolutionary literary history of the Americas" ("Otra vez Caliban," 187). On "Nuestra América" as a forerunner of postcolonial theory, see Lomas, *Translating Empire*. Martí, Lomas argues, is "an uncanny ancestor for some of today's most influential contemporary postcolonial [. . .] theory" (75). On "Nuestra América" as a Latin American alternative to postcolonial theory, see Achugar, "Leones, cazadores e historiadores." For arguments related to Achugar's, see Moraña, "Boom of the Subaltern"; Klor de Alva, "Colonialism and Postcolonialism"; and Mignolo, "Posoccidentalismo." It is worth adding that Martí is often thought to have anticipated a wide range of theories and theorists beyond just the postcolonial: Schulman, for example, writes that "Martí anticipated Foucault's concept of the individual voice of the author" (*Proyecto inconcluso*, 95).

7. Fernández Retamar, *Caliban and Other Essays*, 18. Further references are cited parenthetically in the text.

8. See, for example, Volek, "*Nuestra América* / Our America." Volek claims that "as a work of art, *Nuestra América* cannot be read intrinsically only" be-

cause it is "part of a historical situation" (146). However, Volek also claims that Martí's essay transcends its historical situation because its "core idea of freedom and humanity continues to be our own unsettling and central vital problem" (147–148).

9. Some scholars, however, have begun to question the authority traditionally afforded to Martí and his writings. See, for example, Conway, "Limits of Analogy"; Guerra, *Myth of José Martí*; Morán, *Martí, la justicia infinita*; López, *Future of Cuban Nationalisms*; and Santí, "Crisis of Latinamericanism."

10. José Martí, *Obras completas*, 8:35. Further references are cited parenthetically in the text.

11. On Blaine and the Pan-American Conference, see Healy, *James G. Blaine*; and Soler, *Idea y cuestión*.

12. Loveman, *No Higher Law*, 140.

13. Langley writes that "Creoles read Newton, Locke, Rousseau, Voltaire, Diderot, Montesquieu, and Adam Smith, but it was not the liberating rhetoric of Enlightenment thought driving some of them on a collision course with Spaniards—many of whom were reading the same forbidden tracts—but the reality that they must find a way to enhance opportunity but not jeopardize their property rights" (*Age of Revolution*, 163).

14. Lynch, "Spanish American Independence," 45. On the important role of translations in Latin American independence, see Grases, "Traducciones de interés político-cultural"; and Bastin, Echeverri, and Campo, "Emancipation of Hispanic America."

15. Miranda, *Archivo del General Miranda*, 404, quoted in Onís, *Spanish American Writers*, 22. On Miranda and the United States, see Racine, "Finding the Founding Fathers."

16. Posada and Ibáñez, *Precursor*, 81, quoted in Onís, *Spanish American Writers*, 64. According to Bushnell, "it is likely that Nariño hoped at first only for some liberalization of government within the framework of the Spanish empire" (*Making of Modern Colombia*, 32).

17. Viscardo y Guzmán, "Open Letter to *América*," 61, 64. On Viscardo, see Simmons, *Escritos de Juan Pablo Viscardo y Guzmán*.

18. Ibid., 66.

19. Brading, *First America*, 536, 573. On Latin American responses to European theories regarding the region's inferiority, see Gerbi, "Reaction to de Pauw in Spanish America."

20. See, for example, Rodríguez O., *Independence of Spanish America*; Stoetzer, *Scholastic Roots*; Adelman, *Sovereignty and Revolution*; and Kinsbruner, *Independence in Spanish America*.

21. L. de Zavala, for example, writes in the prologue to his *Viage a los Estados-Unidos* (1834) that "nothing can offer more useful political lessons to my fellow citizens than the knowledge of the customs, uses, habits, and government of the people of the United States, whose institutions we have duti-

fully copied" (*Viage a los Estados-Unidos*, j). For further examples, see Carballo, *¿Qué país es éste?*; and Lipp, *U.S.A.-Spanish America*.

22. Horowitz, "*Federalist* Abroad," 505.

23. Sarmiento, "Conflictos y armonías," 139.

24. Zea, *Pensamiento latinoamericano*, 514.

25. For example, Franco argues that Martí was the first Spanish American writer "to find virtues in the barbarism that European civilisation utterly condemned" (*Spanish American Literature*, 53). Salomon suggests that Martí was "the first to create, line by line, a meaningful and coherent theory of the personality of Spanish America [. . .] free from foreign models" ("José Martí," 223). According to Fernández Retamar, "the work of Martí [. . .] proved too advanced for its context: we would have to wait for the organic insertion of Marxism-Leninism in our America [. . .] for its work to be fully understood and continued" ("América Latina," 319). For Saldívar, "Nuestra América" marked "the beginning of a new epoch of resistance to empire in the Americas" (*Dialectics of Our America*, 7).

26. Burns notes that "by midcentury, if not sooner," many intellectuals "began to voice second thoughts about the impact and forms of progress" (*Poverty of Progress*, 51). After 1850, Burns goes on to note, even Juan Bautista Alberdi "challenged the central premise of the modernizers by denouncing Sarmiento's *Civilización y Barbarie* as invalid," and the Bolivian José Maria Dalence wrote that "many of the Indian groups of his nation exhibited greater intelligence than some Europeans" (53). See also C. A. Hale, *Age of Mora*. He argues that after the Mexican-American War, the problem for Mexican liberals was that their "model nation had turned antagonist" and was not "an ideal liberal progressive society under republican institutions" but an "old-style aggressor, a phenomenon that was assumed to have vanished in the free air of the new world" (207). Mexican liberals thus found themselves unable to "conjure up [. . .] alternative values to replace those that had made North America so strong and irresistible" (209). Although "there was little display of anti-yanquismo among the liberals," the conservative position was that "the United States was not only a threat to Mexican existence, but its culture and its values were not ones Mexico should emulate" (212). In 1853, Hale notes, the newspaper *El Universal* "argued that a Hispanic alliance must be formed to meet the expansive threat of the new northern barbarians" (214).

27. Rojas Mix has argued that Bilbao "not only preceded other thinkers in the use of the expression 'Latin America,' but also anticipated the meaning that the expression would later assume for the Latin American left" ("Bilbao," 38). J. Ramos has also suggested that Bilbao offered a "critique against imperialism that in many ways anticipates post-1898 *Latinoamericanista* discourses" (*Divergent Modernities*, 156). On Torres Caicedo's use of "América Latina," see Ardao, "José María Torres Caicedo."

28. C. A. Hale, "Political Ideas and Ideologies," 138.

29. Billias, *American Constitutionalism*.

30. Echeverría, *Obras escogidas*, 197, quoted in Zea, *Pensamiento latinoamericano*, 155.

31. Zea, *Pensamiento latinoamericano*, 155.

32. Zea, "Positivismo," xxxii.

33. Rodó, *Mirador de Próspero*, 45, quoted in Ardao, *Filosofía en el Uruguay*, 27.

34. Helg, "Race in Argentina and Cuba," 39.

35. Bunge, *Nuestra América*, 139.

36. For a comparison of Martí's views on race with those of Latin American intellectuals such as Agustín Alvarez, Francisco Bulnes, Carlos Octavio Bunge, Alcides Arguedas, and José Ingenieros, see Stabb, "Martí and the Racists."

37. Helg, "Race in Argentina and Cuba," 38.

38. In *Our Rightful Share*, Helg questions not only the extent of Martí's commitment to a raceless universal humanity but also the sincerity of his claim that there was no reason to fear race war in Cuba. She argues that "fear of another Haiti was [. . .] present even in the political thought" of Martí, and points to the "Manifesto de Montecristi," signed by both Martí and Máximo Gómez, which both dismissed fear of the "black race" as "foolish and never justified in Cuba" and validated fears of "a still invisible minority of malcontent freedmen" or of "[black] infamous demagogues" who might incite a race war (54). Helg's Martí is thus not Ferrer's principled idealist whose antiracism is hijacked to silence and squelch black political activism. On the contrary, Helg's Martí is a participant in that silencing.

39. De la Fuente, *Nation for All*, 24.

40. Thomas, *Pursuit of Freedom*, 81.

41. L. A. Pérez, *Between Reform and Revolution*, 103.

42. Ibid.

43. Guerra, *Myth of José Martí*, 9.

44. Ferrer, "Silence of Patriots," 234.

45. Ibid.

46. Ibid.

47. Martí argues that even after the abolition of slavery in Puerto Rico, "there are still many slaves, black and white," thereby deracializing slavery and making it symbiotic with coloniality (318).

48. Michaels has critiqued the tendency to view "the appeal to universality as an attempt to compel agreement" as well as the notion that such attempts conceal "ethnocentric biases" (*Shape of the Signifier*, 31). For Michaels, "the fact that people have locally different views about what is universally true in no way counts as a criticism of the universality of the true" (31). Hence, the "universal does not compel our agreement" but is "implied by our disagreement; and we invoke the universal not to resolve our disagreement but to explain the fact that we disagree" (31). More directly relevant to Martí's "Nuestra

América" is Michaels's point that the replacement of "difference of opinion" with "difference in point of view" makes disagreement impossible (31). The point, he argues, "of the appeal to perspective is that it eliminates disagreement—to see things differently because we see from different perspectives (through different eyes, from different places) is to see the same thing differently but without contradiction" (31). The result is that subject positions become essential, "since to differ without disagreement is nothing more than to occupy a different subject position" (32).

49. Martí, *Versos sencillos / Simple Verses*, 23.

50. Jrade, *Modernismo*, 46.

51. Martí, *Versos sencillos / Simple Verses*, 23.

52. Michaels discusses the idea of "identity as both description and responsibility" (141) in the context of what he calls American "nativist modernism" (*Our America*, 141). His central argument is that all "accounts of cultural identity that do any work require a racial component" (128). In other words, whenever culture is not merely "whatever beliefs and practices we actually happen to have" but rather "the beliefs and practices that [. . .] properly go with the sort of people we happen to be," we will be forced to "appeal to something that must be beyond culture and that cannot be derived from culture precisely because our sense of which culture is properly ours must be derived from it" (128–129). See also Appiah's discussion of the ways in which Du Bois's paper to the American Negro Academy in 1897 on "The Conservation of Races" uses the idea of "common history" as the "allegedly socio-historical" grounds for racial identity and differentiation as opposed to "scientific—that is, biological" ones ("Uncompleted Argument," 25). Even though Du Bois attempts the "transcendence of the nineteenth-century scientific conception of race," Appiah argues that Du Bois ultimately "relies on it" (25).

53. Ortiz, "Martí and the Race Problem," 264.

54. Ibid. Along the same lines, Marinello argued in the 1960s that Martí's attack on race and racism was the result of a "profound humanistic feeling [that] needed to manifest itself against the interested division of mankind based on skin color" (*Obras martianas*, 244). More recently, Rojas noted that he did not see any "signs of essentialist nationalism in Martí" and argued that Martí "thought that any rhetoric of identification with racial, religious, or cultural taints could reinforce the prejudice that the Cuban people were not apt for sovereign government" ("'Otro gallo cantaría,'" 16). For an overview of scholarly accounts of Martí and the question of race, see Fountain, "Martí and Race."

55. Martínez-Echazábal, "Martí and Race: A Re-evaluation," 117.

56. One of the best-known instances of this is Eugenio María de Hostos's "El Cholo," which attempts to eradicate racism through miscegenation, a process that allows a commitment to biological race to remain intact. For a more recent instantiation of this logic, pervasive in Latin American antiracism to this day, see the discussion of the lyrics to José Luís Rodríguez's 1980s song

"Pavo Real" in Hiraldo, *Segregated Miscegenation*. "Pavo Real," Hiraldo suggests, was popular in Latin America because it "celebrates miscegenation" but never "questions the concept of racial hierarchies" and does not "problematize the notion of race itself" (2). On the relationship between hybridity and race, see Lund, *Impure Imagination*. Lund argues that "to theorize hybridity is to operate within a discourse of race" (3).

57. Bronfman, *Measures of Equality*, 187n4.

58. Ferrer, "Silence of Patriots," 244. Ferrer acknowledges elsewhere, however, that Martí's same prohibition on race-thinking and repudiation of racial identity gave blacks in Cuba a "powerful weapon" to combat racism, inasmuch as it allowed racism to be attacked simply on the grounds that it violated the spirit of raceless *cubanidad* (*Insurgent Cuba*, 162). Nevertheless, the main thrust of Ferrer's position is that the language of raceless *cubanidad* not only failed to fulfill black aspirations for social equality but also squelched those aspirations. However, Ferrer fails to show how Martí's language of raceless *cubanidad*, once a "powerful weapon" to abolish racism, becomes complicit with that racism. In other words, Ferrer does not show why only an attack on racism that invokes racial identities has the power to abolish racism.

59. P. C. Taylor, *Race*, 30. Fields and Fields argue in *Racecraft* that "the first principle of racism is the belief in race, even if the believer does not deduce from that belief that the member of a race should be enslaved or disfranchised or shot on sight by trigger-happy police officers [. . .], just as believing that the sun travels around the earth is geocentrism, whether or not one deduces from the belief that persons affirming the contrary should be hauled before an inquisition and forced to recant" (109). "If race lives on today," they argue, "it can do so only because we continue to create and re-create it in our social life, continue to verify it, and thus continue to need a social vocabulary that will allow us to make sense, not of what our ancestors did then, but of what we ourselves choose to do now" (148).

60. Belnap has noted that metaphors of "dress and bodily adornment" in "Nuestra América" are crucial vehicles for Martí's critique of Europeanized Latin American elites ("Headbands, Hemp Sandals, and Headdresses," 193).

61. Lagmanovich, "Lectura de un ensayo," 242.

62. See Alonso, *Spanish American Regional Novel*. Writing broadly about Latin American cultural discourse, Alonso broaches one of the major problems related to the conception of culture in "Nuestra América." He argues that the rhetoric of autochthonous cultural crisis, of which "Nuestra América" is a seminal part, emanates from a profoundly contradictory logic, oscillating between "nostalgia for a relinquished state of cultural plenitude that is associated with an unspecified moment in the past, and the affirmation of the present as a moment that announces proleptically the future cultural redemption" (11). In other words, the rhetoric of cultural crisis "derives its militant force from measuring how far the culture has strayed from its 'true' source; and yet, to make a case for the coextensive nature of the cultural order it envisions

with the culture in question it must also be able to argue that the culture never *really* left there in the first place" (12). For Alonso, the contradiction in essays such as "Nuestra América" is the coexistence of "denunciations of difference and affirmations of immutable self-identity" (12). But what is "immutable self-identity" if not another name for race?

63. P. C. Taylor, *Race*, 48.

64. According to Michaels, what defeats the commitment to culture as an alternative to race is the simultaneous commitment to both culture and pluralism. Pluralism's "programmatic hostility to universalism—its hostility to the idea that cultural practices be justified by appeals to what seems universally good or true—requires that such practices be justified instead by appeals to what seems locally good or true, which is to say, it invokes the identity of the group as the grounds for the justification of the group's practices" (*Our America*, 14). In other words, "the pluralist claim that our practices are justified only because they are better for us requires us to be able to say who we are independent of those practices and so requires us to produce our racial identity" (139). However, the "cultural claim denies the relevance of race and leaves us unable to appeal to facts about who we are as justifications for what we do" (139).

65. Bolívar, *Writings of Simón Bolívar*, 35. Further references are cited parenthetically in the text.

66. Kuper, *Culture*, 240. Kuper notes that "contemporary American anthropologists repudiate the popular ideas that differences are natural, and that cultural identity must be grounded in a primordial, biological identity" (239). He argues, however, that the rhetoric of "difference and identity is not the best placed to counter these views" (239).

67. Balibar, "Is There a 'Neo-Racism'?," 22.

68. Ibid., 24.

69. Quijano, "Modernity, Identity, and Utopia," 149.

70. J. Ramos, *Divergent Modernities*, 264.

71. Appiah, "Identity, Authenticity, Survival," 163.

CHAPTER 2: BELIEFS

1. Rodó, *Ariel*, 31. Further references are cited parenthetically in the text.

2. Zea, *Dialéctica de la conciencia*, 73.

3. Michaels has argued that "beliefs necessarily transcend the person who holds them: to believe that something is true is to believe that it is true for everyone and thus only incidentally true for oneself" (*Shape of the Signifier*, 157). Thus, "the relevant thing about beliefs" is that "they are true or false rather than yours or mine" (38).

4. Michaels argues that "beliefs are intrinsically universal: true (if true) whether or not everyone believes them, false (when false) even if everyone be-

lieves them" (*Shape of the Signifier*, 178). According to Michaels, therein lies the problem with understanding "the difference between one cultural nation and another [. . .] on the model of the difference between ideologies" (41). If we "believe that American values are really better than the next country's," then "their function as a mark of our distinctiveness is jeopardized; other peoples, recognizing the superiority of our beliefs, might be convinced by them and come to share them" (42).

5. Kusch, *Indigenous and Popular Thinking*, 103. Further references are cited parenthetically in the text.

6. Mignolo, *Global Histories/Local Designs*, 6; Mendieta, "Ethics of (Not) Knowing," (263).

7. Henríquez Ureña, *Corrientes literarias*, 183. On the reception of *Ariel*, see Zum Felde, "Promoción intelectual arielista"; and García Morales, "Ariel en México." On *Ariel* and Brazil, see Newcomb, "José Enrique Rodó."

8. On Reyes, Henríquez Ureña, and *Ariel*, see Conn, "Pedagogic and Aesthetic States."

9. Miller, *Reinventing Modernity*, 26. With regard to Rodó's relativism, Miller suggests that "the most significant element that Rodó drew from both Romanticism and positivism was the idea that knowledge is relative," which offered him an "escape route from deterministic views of Latin America" and "provided him with the framework for a challenge to European epistemology, based on a practice of selective appropriation from a variety of cultural movements rather than outright repudiation of any of them" (44).

10. J. Abelardo Ramos, *Historia de la nación*, 83, quoted in Aínsa, *Del canon a la periferia*, 78; García Calderón, *Creación de un continente*, 98, quoted in Real de Azúa, "Prólogo a *Ariel*," xxvi. Other noteworthy critiques of *Ariel* can be found in Sánchez, *Balance y liquidación*; and Rangel, *Latin Americans*. According to Rangel, the problem with *Ariel* was that the notion of leisure that it advanced relied on something unacknowledged by Rodó, namely, "the labor of slaves in the Central American coffee plantations or in the tin mines of Bolivia" (96). For a critical response to Rangel's arguments, see Ardao, "Del mito Ariel al mito anti-Ariel," 117–141.

11. Fernández Retamar, *Caliban and Other Essays*, 14. For a critique of Fernández Retamar's position on *Ariel*, see Rodríguez Monegal, "Metamorfosis de Caliban."

12. Beverley, *Subalternity and Representation*, 18. Specifically, Beverley argued that "what Mabel Moraña and Hugo Achugar invoke against the relevance of subaltern studies and postcolonial theory to Latin America amounts to what I would characterize as a kind of neo-Arielism, to recall José Enrique Rodó's turn-of-the-century characterization of Latin America as Ariel the poet, 'the creature of the air': a reassertion of the authority of Latin American literature, literary criticism, and literary intellectuals like themselves to serve as the bearers of Latin America's cultural memory against forms of thought and theoretical practice identified with the United States" (18). For Beverley,

these positions "entail a kind of unconscious *blanqueamiento* a la Sarmiento, which misrepresents the history and character of even those countries they claim to speak for" (19).

13. On 1898 and its importance for Latin American politics and culture, see Zea and Santana, *1898 y su impacto*; and Bernecker, *1898*.

14. McPherson, *Yankee No!*, 14.

15. McPherson, "*Antiyanquismo*," 14.

16. On Ariel and Caliban in Latin America, see J. T. Reid, "Rise and Decline"; Vaughan, "Caliban"; and Brotherston, "*Arielismo* and Anthropophagy."

17. Darío, "Triunfo de Calibán," 453. On Darío's essay, see Jáuregui, "Calibán, ícono del 98."

18. Ibid.

19. Aínsa, *Del canon a la periferia*, 70. On the idea of the "sick continent" in late nineteenth- and early twentieth-century Latin America, see Stabb, "Sick Continent"; Rojas Mix, "Raza y 'pueblo enfermo'"; and Aronna, "*Pueblos Enfermos*." On the role of the concept of eugenics in debates concerning progress and civilization, see Stepan, *Hour of Eugenics*.

20. Ibid.

21. Mejías-López, *Inverted Conquest*, 46. See also Rojas, "Moral Frontier," 145–160.

22. For a different (but not entirely incompatible) reading of the bronze statue in *Ariel*, see Aching, *Politics of Spanish American Modernismo*.

23. Molloy notes that in "an essay that shuns the visual with passion," the "only visual reference, the only physical detail contained in the essay is therefore all the more striking: gazing at his young disciples [. . .] Prospero pauses to caress the winged statue of Ariel" ("Politics of Posing," 190).

24. I. Zavala, however, argues that *Ariel*'s "openness, diversity, and generic indeterminacies" are the basis for its "counterdiscourse of symbolic resistance" (*Colonialism and Culture*, 99). According to Zavala, *Ariel* participates in "a version of deconstructionist thinking, by which science and logic are denied epistemological privilege and are understood as self-deluding forms of discourse on account of their totalizing truth claims" (99). *Ariel*, Zavala suggests, should be read as "a contingent and open-ended text indicating the pluralization of modern cultural identities" (99). *Ariel*, she argues, is a refusal of the choice between "opposing camps" or "opposing points of view on democracy and technology"; the "unfinalized nature" of *Ariel*'s ending is an attempt to create a space for "the ultimate dialogicality" (102).

25. C. A. Hale, "Political Ideas and Ideologies," 179.

26. Concha, "Youth as *Humano Tesoro*," 112.

27. Ibid., 114.

28. Van Delden, "Survival of the Prettiest," 156.

29. Ibid., 158.

30. See Fouillée, *Mouvement idéaliste*.

31. C. A. Hale, "Political Ideas and Ideologies," 179. Brotherston has simi-

larly noted that Fouillée's *L'idée moderne du droit* was ultimately "more important than either Renan or Shakespeare in the creation of *Ariel*" ("Introduction," 5). See also Pereda, *Rodó's Main Sources*.

32. Concha, "Youth as *Humano Tesoro*," 115, 114.

33. On Fouillée and race, see Staum, "Heredity and Milieu."

34. Fouillée, *Modern French Legal Philosophy*, 17. Further references are cited parenthetically in the text.

35. On Fouillée's concept of "force-ideas," see Kloppenberg, "Philosophy of the *Via Media*."

36. Bagehot, *Physics and Politics*, 36.

37. Rachels, "Challenge of Cultural Relativism," 153. Further references are cited parenthetically in the text.

38. On this point, see Boghossian, "Objective Epistemic Reasons." If, Boghossian argues, "no evidential system is more correct than any other, then I cannot coherently think that a particular belief is blameworthy, no matter how crazy *it* may be, so long as that belief is grounded in a set of [. . .] epistemic norms that permit it, no matter how crazy *they* may be" (253). In other words, as long as we believe that "there is nothing that epistemically privileges one set of epistemic principles over another," we cannot disagree, and "it becomes impossible to evade some sort of relativistic upshot" (253).

39. Castro-Gómez, "Missing Chapter of Empire," 282, 298.

40. González Echevarría, "Case of the Speaking Statue," 19.

41. Ibid., 19–20.

42. Ibid., 20. For González Echevarría, this is the "founding fiction" of *Ariel*, namely, that "it is a dialogue, not a speech; a seminar, not a lecture" (20). There is, after all, "no dialogic exchange in the essay," but the "dialoguelike setting" functions to secure, he argues, the "masterly and magisterial position" of the teacher and the "subservient position" of the mute reader (21).

43. See, for example, Forjas, *Cosmopolitanism in the Americas*.

44. González Echevarría, "Case of the Speaking Statue," 25.

45. Aching, *Politics of Spanish American Modernismo*, 27.

46. Salles, "Rodó, Race, and Morality," 191.

47. Ibid., 192.

48. Mignolo, *Darker Side of the Renaissance*, 252.

49. Groff, *Critical Realism*, 135.

50. Boghossian, *Fear of Knowledge*, 2. Further references are cited parenthetically in the text.

51. On Kusch's *ser/estar* distinction, see Fornet-Betancourt, *Estudios de filosofía latinoamericana*, 97–100; and Mignolo, "Occidentalización, imperialismo, globalización."

52. Wallerstein, *Historical Capitalism*, 81. Further references are cited parenthetically in the text.

53. Balibar, "Racism as Universalism," 198.

54. Ibid., 202.

55. Ibid., 204.

56. Davidson, "Truth Rehabilitated," 72.

57. Ibid.

58. Ibid.

59. In *Mirror of Nature*, Rorty argued that in the disagreement between Copernicus and Cardinal Bellarmine, it is impossible to "find a way of saying that the considerations advanced against the Copernican theory by Cardinal Bellarmine [. . .] were 'illogical or unscientific'" (328). For Rorty, "the crucial consideration is whether we know how to draw a line between science and theology such that getting the heavens right is a 'scientific' value, and preserving the church, and the general cultural structure of Europe, is an 'unscientific' value" (329). Today most people would argue that "scripture is *not* an excellent source of evidence for the way the heavens are set up," but that is only because, Rorty suggests, they have absorbed "three hundred years of rhetoric about the importance of distinguishing sharply between science and religion, science and politics, science and art, science and philosophy" (329–330).

60. Ibid., 77.

61. Ibid. See also Bernstein, "Conversation of Mankind."

62. Fish, "Liberalism Doesn't Exist," 136.

63. Fish, *Trouble with Principle*, 268.

64. Fish, "Foreword," xviii.

65. In "Fixation of Belief" (1877), Peirce declared that "the most that can be maintained is, that we seek for a belief that we shall *think* to be true," and that it is "mere tautology" to say that we "think each one of our beliefs to be true" (*Philosophical Writings*, 10–11).

66. Haack, *Evidence and Inquiry*, 250.

67. Ibid.

68. See Roig, *Teoría y crítica*; and Miró Quesada, *Proyecto de filosofar latino-americano*.

69. Salazar Bondy, *¿Existe una filosofía de nuestra América?*, 82. Further references are cited parenthetically in the text.

70. For a discussion of this debate, see Cerutti Guldberg, *Filosofía de la liberación*; Gallardo, "Pensar en América Latina"; and Dussel, "Philosophy in Latin America."

71. Mignolo, "Immigrant Consciousness," xiv.

CHAPTER 3: MEANING

1. In his essay on Latin American *testimonio* from the late 1980s, Beverley laments the fact that "our very notions of literature and the literary are bound up with notions of the author, or, at least, of an authorial intention" and celebrates *testimonio* because it "involves a sort of erasure of the function, and thus also of the textual presence, of the 'author'" (*Testimonio*, 35). Sorensen Good-

rich argues in the introduction to her 1996 book on *Facundo* that a text "is an object for the active reading subject, who is a creative coproducer in a communication process that is not subordinated to the notion of a correct or appropriate interpretation" (*Facundo*, 3). Thus, she argues, given that "there is no such thing as the objective meaning of a work," the "varied readings" of *Facundo* "can be said to constitute its meaning" (4). Masiello celebrates the poetry of Néstor Perlongher for the ways in which it challenges "lines of signification that have sustained rigid hierarchies of meaning" and makes language "physical to the detriment of meaning" (*Art of Transition*, 70). Dove declares that "reading does not happen at the level of the narrator's or writer's intention, i.e., as the communication of information and meaning from writer to reader; rather, it takes place at those points of a story or history that exceed the comprehension of the one who narrates" (*Catastrophe of Modernity*, 230). Most recently, Graff Zivin complains that readings of allegory tend to rely "on an outmoded understanding of, among other things, the idea of authorial intent, the transparency of language, and the link between signifier and signified" (*Figurative Inquisitions*, 61). Graff Zivin proposes that we view a text's allegorical meaning not as the function of the intention of the author but instead as the product of the desire of the reader: what makes a text allegorical, she argues, is that "the reader *desires* such a relationship" (62).

2. Rama, *Lettered City*, 39, 58–59.

3. Graff Zivin, "Introduction: Reading Otherwise," 2.

4. Ibid.

5. See, for example, Sorensen Goodrich, *Reader and the Text*.

6. Cortázar, *Blow-Up and Other Stories*, 64–65. Of course, the participation of the reader is often thought to be central to Cortázar's fiction in general: for Ortega, in a novel such as *Hopscotch* "the characters are [. . .] readers and the reader is a character" (*Poetics of Change*, 42).

7. As Sauri argues, "our reactions to persons, things, or ideas are in no way constitutive of what we believe about them. And while our experiences may no doubt inform those beliefs, these remain irreducible to any account of the manner in which we come to have them. Indeed, no individual is 'convinced' when he or she has an experience, inasmuch as that experience is nothing more than the effect created by a particular stimulus" ("Literary Form," 410–411). The effort to link the interpretation of the text to a reader's experience of the text, Sauri argues, ultimately means that "any interpretation of a given text constitutes nothing but an account of a particular reader's experience" (410).

8. Henríquez Ureña, *Seis ensayos*, 243.

9. This is not to say that Borges does not advance other accounts of meaning across his work that contradict with "Pierre Menard." In "Detective Story" (1978), for example, Borges argues that "literary genres may depend less on texts than on the way texts are read"; he writes that a book "begins to exist when a reader opens it," hence its meaning "requires the conjunction of reader and text" (491–492).

10. Block de Behar, *Rhetoric of Silence*, 48; Molloy, *Signs of Borges*, 31. Alonso is one of the few critics to recognize that Borges's story depends not on the contexts of reading but on the replacement of one author for another. "Pierre Menard," Alonso argues, is about "what happens when we begin a process of reading with Menard in the place previously occupied by Cervantes" ("Borges y la teoría," 446). The answer, Alonso states, "is that nothing is the same" because the narrator produces an "impeccable reading of the fragment from the first part of *Don Quixote* that is no less convincing and 'correct' than previous interpretations that presumed that Cervantes was the author of the novel" (445). For Alonso, "to read the *Quixote* we must first create the figure of an author in order to decode the text" (445). "We are used to using a figure that we know by the name of 'Cervantes' in that procedure," Alonso notes, but "it becomes clear that another authorial figure" can occupy that place, in which case everything changes (446).

11. For a reading of "Pierre Menard" based on the sources and references in the story, see Balderston, *Out of Context*.

12. Borges, *Labyrinths*, 39. Further references are cited parenthetically in the text.

13. On the role of belief in "Pierre Menard," see Johnson, *Kant's Dog*. Johnson is correct when he affirms that the "investment in the origin, the original, and the author" depends on "belief" (47). To "attribute Mme. Henri Bachelier's *Le jardin du centaure* to Madame Henri Bachelier as if she had authored it" is for us to believe that she authored it (85). Additionally, Johnson rightly challenges the claim that "the difference between Menard and Cervantes is contextually determined"; those who make that claim, he argues, "do not ask what makes possible the determination of contextual or historical authority, that is, what makes possible such authorization and such attribution" (238). However, Johnson's understanding of belief depends on a Humean skepticism that leads him to collapse the distinction between (sensory) experience and belief, with the result that truth becomes contingent on the believing subject.

14. See Knapp and Michaels, "Not a Matter of Interpretation," where "Pierre Menard" is briefly invoked in the service of a critique of U.S. Supreme Court Justice Antonin Scalia's "textualist" theory of statutory interpretation. It goes without saying that "Pierre Menard" has been invoked to support a wide range of theoretical claims and perspectives. See, for example, Blanchot, *Book to Come*; Derrida, *Ear of the Other*; Jauss, "Theory of Reception"; Rodríguez Monegal, "Borges and Derrida"; Danto, *Transfiguration of the Commonplace*; Steiner, *After Babel*; Arrojo, "Translation, Transference, and the Attraction to Otherness"; Hayles, "Translating Media"; and D. I. Pérez, "Ontology of Art."

15. Knapp and Michaels, "Against Theory," 725. Further references are cited parenthetically in the text. See also Michaels's discussion of the ways in which seeing "difference as disagreement makes the subject position of the observer irrelevant (since to disagree with someone is to produce a judgment that, if it is true, is true also for the person with whom you disagree—that's

why we think of ourselves as disagreeing)," whereas "difference without disagreement makes the subject position essential (since to differ without disagreeing is nothing more than to occupy a different position)" (*Shape of the Signifier*, 32).

16. For an argument to the contrary, see McGann, *Textual Condition*; and the responses to the Michaels and Knapp argument in Mitchell, *Against Theory*.

17. Sacerío-Gari argues that "Pierre Menard" affirms not a distinction between "the *actions* of producers and the *reactions* of consumers," but the opposite ("Towards Pierre Menard," 467). See also Genette, *Palimpsests*. For Genette, "Borges succeeded in demonstrating with the imaginary example of Pierre Menard that the mere displacement of context turns even the most literal rewriting into a creation" (17).

18. Sarlo, *Jorge Luis Borges*, 32.

19. Ibid., 33. See also Waisman, *Borges and Translation*. Waisman makes a similar argument when he suggests that "Pierre Menard" teaches us "that through changes in the context, even the same words in the same language can gain entirely new meanings—and that this can occur, paradoxically, without necessarily losing the old meanings" (15).

20. Fernández Retamar, *Caliban and Other Essays*, 86. Further references are cited parenthetically in the text.

21. For a discussion of Retamar's essay, see Palermo, "De apropiaciones y desplazamientos," 181–198. A more critical perspective can be found in Moreiras's *Tercer espacio*.

22. González Echevarría, "Brief History," 8.

23. See also, for example, Benedetti, *Ejercicio del criterio*. In his essay on the differences between Vallejo and Neruda, Benedetti suggested that the difference between the two poets was the location of what mattered about their work: for Neruda, wrote Benedetti, "the most important thing is the poem itself," whereas for Vallejo, "the most important thing is usually what is before (or behind) the poem" (119).

24. Rodó, *Rubén Darío*, 11, 10.

25. Ibid.

26. Vargas Llosa, "Social Commitment," 6. Further references are cited parenthetically in the text.

27. In his 1973 essay "Para una teoría de la literatura hispanoamericana," reprinted in his book of the same title, Fernández Retamar wrote that because there "still is not one single world," there is "naturally still no general or world literature" (*Para una teoría*, 79). Thus, "if the object in question (world literature) does not yet exist, how can that object be theorized, contemplated, or revealed?" (79). In 1976, however, he celebrated the "recent incorporation of Latin American literature into world literature" because it is evidence of "a widening of the real horizon of humanity" and "prioritizes the enormously richer vision we are constructing throughout the planet, according to which

essential human beings are also female, black [and] yellow" (*Para una teoría*, 235). Fernández Retamar thus embraces the universal (which he understands as synonymous with globality) because it reveals difference and makes it essential.

28. In *Shape of the Signifier*, Michaels argues that once ideas in a text count "not because some author meant them to count but because they are there, in front of you, then everything that is there must count—the table the pages are on, the room the table is in, the way the pages, the table, and the room make you feel" (11). That is because, Michaels shows, "once we abjure interest in what the author intended," then "we have no principled reason not to count everything that's part of our experience as part of the work" (11). Fish makes the same point in *Doing What Comes Naturally* when he argues that "the abandonment of formalism—of the derivation of meaning from mechanically enumerable features—has always and already occurred" (7); for Fish, the very act of looking at a text as "meaningful," which is to say, as a text in the first place, "is already to have posited for it an intention (by assuming the intentional circumstances of its production)" (118).

29. Quoted in Jackson, *Black Literature and Humanism*, 10.

30. In *Postmodernity in Latin America*, Colás critiques, for example, what he sees as the "unconscious universalizing impulses" (4) in Linda Hutcheon's *Poetics of Postmodernism* (1987). Colás notes that because Hutcheon's definition of postmodernism is based exclusively on formal "techniques" (1), it results in a "misappropriation of Latin American fiction for her transnational canon of postmodern historiographic fiction" (3). In other words, because postmodernism for Hutcheon is merely the sum of "techniques such as the manipulation of narrative perspective, self-consciousness, and the incorporation of actual historical figures and texts to challenge the illusion of unified and coherent subjective identity" (1), the difference between, for example, Gabriel García Márquez's *One Hundred Years of Solitude* and Salman Rushdie's *Midnight's Children* begins to disappear. The point is that a text's formal properties will never reveal its cultural specificity in a clear and meaningful way. Thus, Colás points out that Hutcheon's investment in the "stylistic features" (3) that define postmodernism results in her blindness to "local circumstances" and "cultural traditions" (4). Indeed, only an account of "what function these various stylistic features serve" (3) or an account of "the concrete ways these texts may reproduce or be resistant to the dominant economic, political, and cultural institutions in both the First World and the various regions of Latin America" (4) can effectively challenge their "inclusion in [Hutcheon's] canon of postmodernism" (4).

31. Sarlo, *Jorge Luis Borges*, 33.

32. Ibid.

33. Ibid.

34. De la Campa, *Latin Americanism*, x. Further references are cited par-

enthetically in the text. For an incisive critique of de la Campa's *Latin Americanism*, see Levinson, *Ends of Literature*. Levinson argues that "Latin Americanism [. . .], both the version de la Campa practices and the one he critiques, is strongly bound to *theory*: not to deconstruction, structuralism, feminism, or Marxism, etc., but to theory itself" (173). That is because, Levinson argues, "only the appeal to theory can put in question *all* of the following: (1) the developmentalist paradigm that contends that the Other cannot think; (2) liberal humanism, which claims to approach the Latin American topos without theory [. . .]; and (3) deconstructive practices, coming from abroad and not quite fit for Latin America: these can be exposed only by the Latin Americanist *theorist*" (173).

35. Martí, *Selected Writings*, 288–289.

36. Kalimán, "Sobre la construcción del objeto," 307. Further references are cited parenthetically in the text.

37. Paz, "Poesía en movimiento," 34. Further references are cited parenthetically in the text.

38. Leal, *Luis Leal Reader*, 189.

39. Castañón, *América sintaxis*, 334. Paz had already launched a critique of Castro Leal's anthology for its putative commitment to national and social concerns over poetic and aesthetic ones; see Paz's essay "Poesía mexicana moderna" (1957).

40. In *Dissenting Voice*, Stabb notes that the generation of Mexican writers and intellectuals that emerged in the 1960s was largely uninterested in questions of "self-knowledge" and the "Philosophy of Mexicanness" that had loomed large "in the writings of Paz and the Hiperión group of the preceding decade" (13).

41. The titles of other anthologies from this period suggest that *Poesía en movimiento* was somewhat unique in its anxiety about the possibly national essentialist implications of a single-nation anthology, e.g., *Novísima poesía cubana* (1962), *Antología de la poesía peruana* (1965), *La poesía mexicana del siglo XX* (1966), *36 años de poesía uruguaya* (1967), *Panorama de la poesía cubana moderna* (1967), *Antología de la poesía chilena contemporánea* (1968), *Antología lineal de la poesía argentina* (1968).

42. Henríquez Ureña, *Corrientes literarias*, 9.

43. Paz, *Bow and the Lyre*, 261.

44. See Wilson, *Octavio Paz*, for an account of Paz's various efforts to incorporate the experience of the reader into the text of his poems. In reference to Paz's *Las perlas del olmo* (1957), for example, Wilson suggests that Paz understands poetry as a "*seed* of energy" in which "it is up to the reader whether it grows or not" (126); he suggests that in *La estación violenta* (1958), the poem is understood as something "that 'seeds' itself in the reader" (92). See also Alazraki, "Poetry as Coded Silence." Alazraki explores the ways in which Paz (in *Salamandra*) embraces "the notion that reading a poem is a creative (or recreative) exercise" (157).

45. Paz, *Bow and the Lyre*, 26.

46. Ibid., 25.

47. Indeed, it was precisely the difference between an object and a representation that was at stake in Fried's landmark 1967 essay, "Art and Objecthood." Fried was writing about the "enterprise known variously as Minimal Art, ABC Art, Primary Structures, and Specific Objects" (148). That enterprise, he argued, was based on an anxiety about the representative nature of painting—what he called painting's "relational character" and the "inescapability" of its "pictorial illusion" (149). In other words, the "enterprise" Fried writes about involved a choice between "shape as a fundamental property of objects and shape as a medium of painting" (151). The choice—in the work of artists such as Donald Judd and Tony Smith—was toward objects. Fried quotes Judd himself, who talked about two fundamentally different ways of thinking about painting: as a representation, which means the painting has "a limit" (149), or as an object, a rectangle, and not a representation at all, which means the "rectangular plane is given a life span" (149). Fried's point was that although "modernist painting" found it "imperative that it defeat or suspend its own objecthood" (151) by its "relational character" and through "pictorial illusion" (149), literalism "aspires not to defeat or suspend its own objecthood, but on the contrary to discover and project objecthood as such" (151). Thus, according to Fried, literalism does not seek to "represent, signify, or allude to anything" (165). The works "are what they are and nothing more" (165). The trouble with this way of understanding art, Fried argues, is not only that it is the negation of art, but also that it exchanges meaning for experience: in a representation, what matters is a work's meaning and its referential quality, whereas in an object, there is only our experience of it. Given that our experience of an object occurs in space and time, Fried argues, there is nothing "that declares its irrelevance to the situation, and therefore to the experience in question" (155). As a result, everything counts as part of the work of art, "including, it seems, the beholder's *body*" (155). For an account of Fried's distinctions in specifically Marxist terms, see Brown, "Real Subsumption under Capital." Brown argues that "everything Fried finds objectionable in the 'object' is on the other hand perfectly legitimate for a certain class of objects we are already familiar with, namely, commodities. Or, to put this another way, Fried's 'formalist' account of the distinction between art and non-art is also an historicist one, fully derivable from the Marxian problematic of the 'real subsumption of labor under capital,' or the closure of the world market." See also Di Stefano and Sauri, "Making It Visible." The authors argue that "contemporary Latin American studies points to a particular configuration of art's relationship to politics and the market, but one which is predicated on a repudiation of the distinction between literary and non-literary objects, predicated, in other words, on the elimination of the frame." That configuration, they argue, "finds its origins in a transformation in the global structure of exploitation, one which has animated a political concern with categories like ex-

clusion, but which in so doing, has ultimately oriented political theory away from the critique of this same economic structure." Whereas the dissolution of the distinction "between meaning and effect, art and objecthood, and interpretation and experience" participates in the "disavowal of structure (economic, political, social) that neoliberalism demands, the maintenance of that distinction"—by means of "the assertion of the frame"—"preserves the possibility of seeing the very structure of exploitation that neoliberalism demands to be hidden."

48. Cornejo Polar, *Writing in the Air*, 14. Further references are cited parenthetically in the text.

49. Mignolo, *Darker Side of the Renaissance*, 331. Further references are cited parenthetically in the text.

50. For a critique of the idea that making a true claim about the world necessarily involves people being able to stand outside themselves, see Fish, "Reply." The fact that we cannot justify our epistemic system from outside of it, Fish argues, should not lead us to conclude that the beliefs that emerge from our epistemic system might somehow not be true. If "our convictions cannot be grounded in any independent source of authority," it does not mean "our convictions are ungrounded" (925–926). On the contrary, Fish argues that the "unavailability of independent grounds—of foundations that are general and universal rather than local and contextual—is fraught with no implications at all" (926). "It turns out," Fish writes, "that not only are the grounds that are ours by virtue of the resources a lifetime has given us sufficient [. . .] but also they are superior to the independent grounds no one has ever been able to find" (926). See also Trigg, *Reason and Commitment*.

51. See Ashton, *From Modernism to Postmodernism*. Ashton argues that "when words become marks [. . .] we have no choice but to experience them because— if we want to continue to apprehend them as material objects—we can no longer continue to think of ourselves as reading them. That is, we can no longer think of ourselves as reading them because we can no longer think of them as language" (92).

52. Sommer, *Proceed with Caution*, 77. Further references are cited parenthetically in the text.

53. For an important critique of Sommer's main arguments, see Acosta, *Thresholds of Illiteracy*. Acosta rightly recognizes the ways in which Sommer's particularist project necessarily entails a form of universalism, arguing that "the 'paradigm shift' that Sommer announces in the name of a particularist hermeneutic of resistance inevitably leads to the founding of yet another paradigm that will itself seek to overtake the current one" (18). For Acosta, in other words, the problem with *Proceed with Caution* is that "it reads both particularism and universalism as simply competing ideological models of interpretation and ultimately calls for the unseating of universalist reading as hegemonic model and the installing of a particularist ideology in its place" (18). The result, then, is that "the very question of hegemony itself goes unre-

marked" (18). Acosta, however, does not read the contradictions in *Proceed with Caution* as signaling the impossibility of overcoming the universal but rather seeks to establish a model in which "irrespective of authorship, writing itself can bring about its own form of incommensurability, resistance, and indeterminacy" (19). To that end, he develops the concept of "illiteracy," by which he means "the condition of semiological excess and ungovernability that emerges from the critical disruption of the field of intelligibility within which traditional and resistant modes of reading are defined and positioned" (9). Ultimately, Acosta proposes, this results in a nullification of the "very opposition" between "ideologically opposed reading strategies" and a vacating of "the very terms of dispute over which competing ideological claims are made" (9).

54. On the ways in which the relationship between the reader (or spectator) and a work's meaning was a central and recurring preoccupation for modernism, see Siraganian, *Modernism's Other Work*.

55. Beverley, *Subalternity and Representation*, 24.

CHAPTER 4: MEMORY

1. Bonfil Batalla, *México Profundo*, 57, 3. Further references are cited parenthetically in the text.

2. For a critique of Bonfil Batalla's argument, see Lomnitz-Adler, *Deep Mexico*. Lomnitz-Adler notes that "Bonfil does not offer a detailed formulation of the dialectics that have existed between so-called tradition and modernity since the inception of a modern mentality in the late eighteenth century or since the inception of capitalism in the sixteenth century" (264). The "worrisome consequence" of this, he argues, "is that the political application of the 'deep versus invented' imagery must ultimately rely on a system of refined discriminations wherein certain privileged subjects, usually nationally recognized intellectuals or politicians, are placed in a position of interpreting the true national sentiment" (264). Even worse, because Bonfil's notion of a "deep Mexico" cannot "extract Mexico from the world capitalist system," it "tends to re-create or revitalize the sort of authoritarian nationalism that was characteristic of the period of growth under import substitution, a nationalism that [. . .] is bankrupt as a viable political formula today" (264). In *Rise of the Rich*, Gran argues that Bonfil sees "ethnicity and culture" as "racially fixed" (43). From the perspective of political economy, Gran argues, "*México Profundo* naturally is ahistorical; it interprets race in an essentializing way, missing the key point that race itself is simply part of a larger set of historically contingent and interrelated constructions" (43).

3. Michaels has argued that without "the idea of a history that is remembered or forgotten (not merely learned or unlearned), the events of the past can have only a limited relevance to the present, providing us at best with causal accounts of how things have come to be the way they are, at worst with

objects of antiquarian interest" (*Shape of the Signifier*, 138–139). If history is merely something that is learned, Michaels argues, "no history could be more truly ours than any other," and "no history, except the things that had actually happened to us, would be truly ours at all" (139). Instead, it is "only when the events of the past can be imagined not only to have consequences for the present but to *live on* in the present that they can become part of our experience and testify to who we are" (139).

4. See, for example, Achugar, "Presente del pasado."

5. D. Taylor, *Archive and the Repertoire*, xvi. Further references are cited parenthetically in the text.

6. Anderson and Garber, *Fifty Years of Change*, 152–153. See also Dussel Peters, *Polarizing Mexico*; and Otero, "Neoliberal Reform and Politics."

7. Lorenzano, "Angels among Ruins," 250–251.

8. For a related argument to which I am indebted, see Di Stefano, "Shopping Malls to Memory Museums." Di Stefano argues that "the dominant form of memory politics today, insofar as it reframes the critique of capitalism into a critique of authoritarianism, functions as a primary mechanism by which the Left contributes to the expansion of neoliberalism." In other words, Di Stefano argues, it is not the indifference to memory and its so-called erasure that "advances the Uruguayan neoliberal agenda, but rather the commitment to a politics of memory through which the Left increasingly comes to disarticulate its past commitment to economic equality that does so." See also the related discussion in Draper, *Afterlives of Confinement*. Specifically, Draper explores the ways in which "a surplus [. . .] of controlled memory" actually conceals a "selective forgetfulness," or the ways in which the seeming "overabundance of memory and memorials" conceals exclusions performed "by the market and by both left- and right-wing policies" (17).

9. Alonso, *Spanish American Regional Novel*, 12. Further references are cited parenthetically in the text.

10. Martí, *Selected Writings*, 293

11. Gamio, *Forjando patria*, 154.

12. Guillén, *Obra poética*, 1:114.

13. Mariátegui, *Seven Interpretive Essays*, 3, 35–36, 33.

14. Paz, "Mexico and the United States," 362. Paz's investment in the presence of these "old beliefs" was that they were markers of a "continuity, which goes back two thousand years" (363). For Paz, culture is what makes the precolonial past part of the past of present-day Mexicans. However, as Michaels argues, culture alone is not enough to achieve this: the "fact that some people before you did some things that you do does not in itself make what they did part of your past" ("Race into Culture," 680). "To make what *they* did part of *your* past," argues Michaels, "there must be some prior assumption of identity between you and them, and this assumption is [. . .] racial" (680).

15. Ibid.

16. Larrain, *Identity and Modernity*, 172.

17. Ibid.

18. Brewster, *Responding to Crisis*, 150. For a discussion of the transformations within the discourse of Mexican national identity and distinctiveness in the years surrounding the ratification of NAFTA, see Morris, "Neo-liberalism and Neo-indigenismo."

19. Gamio, *Forjando patria*, 25; García Canclini, *Consumers and Citizens*, 114.

20. Rodríguez and Fortier, *Cultural Memory*, 4.

21. Ibid.

22. Ibid. The authors go on to recall a conversation with "a colleague and Nahuatl scholar" who "says that we Mexican Americans do not think or reflect on the meaning of Our Lady of Guadalupe, in much the same way that we do not think of the blood that runs through our veins" (5).

23. Steger and Roy, *Neoliberalism*, 53.

24. Michaels, *Trouble with Diversity*, 172–173.

25. Ibid., 161–162.

26. C. R. Hale, "Does Multiculturalism Menace?," 487.

27. Ibid., 494. On similar constitutional reforms in the region and their provisions for language recognition and multiculturalism, see Van Cott, *Friendly Liquidation*.

28. Ibid., 493.

29. Quoted in García Canclini, "North Americans or Latin Americans?," 143.

30. Portuondo, *Crítica de la época*, 26, quoted in Schulman, "Introduction," 8.

31. Ibid.

32. Jörgensen, *Writings of Elena Poniatowska*, 78–79.

33. "Argentina: *Nunca Más*," 6.

34. Ibid.

35. Crenzel, "Between the Voices," 1063. Further references are cited parenthetically in the text.

36. Klein, "On the Emergence of *Memory*," 130.

37. Ibid.

38. Viotti da Costa, "New Publics, New Politics," 21.

39. Ibid.

40. Quoted in Mazzei, *Death Squads*, 57.

41. Quoted in Kovic, *Mayan Voices*, 189.

42. Rabasa, *Without History*, 233. Further references are cited parenthetically in the text.

43. Sarlo, *Tiempo pasado*, 23. Further references are cited parenthetically in the text.

44. Beverley, "Neoconservative Turn," 65. Further references are cited parenthetically in the text.

45. Beverley, *Testimonio*, 7.

46. Ibid.

47. De Man, "Autobiography as De-facement," 920.

48. Derrida, *Ear of the Other*, 51.

49. Galeano, *Genesis*, xv. Further references are cited parenthetically in the text.

50. Verdesio, "Amnesiac Nation," 202. Further references are cited parenthetically in the text.

51. Franco, *Decline and Fall*, 236–237.

52. Ibid., 237.

53. Olick, Vinitzky-Seroussi, and Levy, "Introduction," 19.

54. Ibid.

55. Austin, *How to Do Things with Words*, 6, quoted in D. Taylor, *Archive and the Repertoire*, 5.

56. Menton, *New Historical Novel*, 14. Further references are cited parenthetically in the text.

57. Williams, *Postmodern Novel*, 5, 19.

58. Adorno, *Polemics of Possession*, 277.

59. Michaels argues that if "what you want is a 'link' with the dead that is better achieved by speaking with them than by studying them [. . .] then the discovery that what one hears when one hears the dead speak is actually the sound of one's 'own voice' can't really count as a disappointment" (*Shape of the Signifier*, 138).

60. Jenkins, *Rethinking History*, 15.

61. Ibid., 14.

62. Boullosa, *Cielos de la tierra*, 32, 16. Further references are cited parenthetically in the text. On Boullosa's novel, see also Hind, "Historical Arguments"; López-Lozano, "Dream of Mestizo Mexico"; Estrada, "(Re)Constructions of Memory"; A. Reid, "Disintegration, Dismemberment, and Discovery"; and the essays collected in Dröscher and Rincón, *Acercamientos a Boullosa*.

63. Hutcheon, *Poetics of Postmodernism*, 111, 113.

64. Ibid., 119.

65. Ibid., 112.

66. Franco, *Cruel Modernity*, 212. Further references are cited parenthetically in the text.

CODA: A NEW LATIN AMERICANISM?

1. Beverley, *Latinamericanism after 9/11*, 6, 8. Further references are cited parenthetically in the text.

2. Van Cott, "Constitutional Reform in the Andes," 45.

3. Ibid., 47.

4. Ibid.

5. Ibid.

6. Albó, "Ethnic Identity and Politics," 26.

7. Ibid.

8. Ibid.

9. MacLeod, *Downsizing the State*, 100, quoted in Harvey, *Brief History of Neoliberalism*, 103.

10. Central Intelligence Agency, *World Factbook: Mexico*, https://www.cia.gov/library/publications/the-world-factbook/geos/mx.html.

11. Sutcliffe, "World Inequality and Globalization," 24.

12. Beverley, *Testimonio*, 7.

13. As with many of the main arguments in *Latinamericanism after 9/11*, this recalls Beverley's work in *Subalternity and Representation*. In that book, he argued that "the project of the left, to the extent that it embodies subaltern will and agency, has to be posed paradoxically as a defense of the nation-state, rather than as something that is 'against' or 'beyond' the nation-state. Of course, what is entailed in this defense is also [. . .] the need for a new kind of state" (153).

14. Salazar Bondy, *¿Existe una filosofía de nuestra América?*, 9.

15. Fraser, *Justice Interruptus*, 13. Further references are cited parenthetically in the text.

16. Michaels, *Trouble with Diversity*, 83. Further references are cited parenthetically in the text.

17. Michaels, *Shape of the Signifier*, 164.

18. Martínez Novo, *Who Defines Indigenous?*, 110. Further references are cited parenthetically in the text.

Bibliography

Aching, Gerard. *The Politics of Spanish American* Modernismo: *By Exquisite Design.* Cambridge: Cambridge University Press, 1997.

Achugar, Hugo. "Leones, cazadores e historiadores, a propósito de las políticas de la memoria y del conocimiento." *Revista Iberoamericana* 63, no. 180 (1997): 379–387.

———. "El presente del pasado, o balance y liquidación de la nación." *Papeles de Montevideo* 2 (1997): 110–124.

Acosta, Abraham. *Thresholds of Illiteracy: Theory, Latin America, and the Crisis of Resistance.* New York: Fordham University Press, 2014.

Adelman, Jeremy. *Sovereignty and Revolution in the Iberian Atlantic.* Princeton, NJ: Princeton University Press, 2006.

Adorno, Rolena. *The Polemics of Possession in Spanish American Narrative.* New Haven, CT: Yale University Press, 2007.

Aínsa, Fernando. *Del canon a la periferia: Encuentros y transgresiones en la literatura uruguaya.* Montevideo: Ediciones Trilce, 2002.

Alazraki, Jaime. "Octavio Paz—Poetry as Coded Silence." In *Octavio Paz*, edited by Harold Bloom, 147–172. Broomall, PA: Chelsea House, 2002.

Albó, Xavier. "Ethnic Identity and Politics in the Central Andes: The Cases of Bolivia, Ecuador, and Peru." In *Politics in the Andes: Identity, Conflict, Reform*, edited by Jo-Marie Burt and Philip Mauceri, 17–37. Pittsburgh, PA: University of Pittsburgh Press, 2004.

Almarza, Sara. "La frase 'Nuestra América': Historia y significado." *Cahiers du monde hispanique et luso-brésilien*, no. 43 (1984): 5–22.

Alonso, Carlos. "Borges y la teoría." *MLN* 120, no. 2 (2005): 437–456.

———. *The Spanish American Regional Novel: Modernity and Autochthony.* Cambridge: Cambridge University Press, 1990.

Anderson, Joan B., and James Garner. *Fifty Years of Change on the U.S.-Mexico Border: Growth, Development, and Quality of Life.* Austin: University of Texas Press, 2008.

Appiah, Kwame Anthony. "Identity, Authenticity, Survival." In *Multiculturalism: Examining the Politics of Recognition*, edited by Amy Gutmann, 149–163. Princeton, NJ: Princeton University Press, 1994.

———. *In My Father's House: Africa in the Philosophy of Culture*. Oxford: Oxford University Press, 1992.

———. "The Uncompleted Argument: Du Bois and the Illusion of Race." *Critical Inquiry* 12, no. 1 (1985): 21–37.

Ardao, Arturo. "Del mito de Ariel al mito anti-Ariel." In *Nuestra América Latina*, 117–144. Montevideo: Ediciones Banda Oriental, 1986.

———. *La filosofía en el Uruguay en el siglo XX*. Mexico City: Fondo de Cultura Económica, 1956.

———. "El nombre 'América Latina': José María Torres Caicedo." In *América Latina y la latinidad*, 53–73. Mexico City: Universidad Nacional Autónoma de México, 1993.

"Argentina: *Nunca Más*—Report of the Argentine Commission on the Disappeared." In *Transitional Justice: How Emerging Democracies Reckon with Former Regimes*, vol. 3, *Laws, Rulings, and Reports*, edited by Neil J. Kritz, 3–47. Washington, DC: United States Institute of Peace, 1995.

Aronna, Michael. *"Pueblos Enfermos": The Discourse of Illness in the Turn-of-the-Century Spanish and Latin American Essay*. Chapel Hill: North Carolina Studies in the Romance Languages and Literatures, 1999.

Arrojo, Rosemary. "Translation, Transference, and the Attraction to Otherness—Borges, Menard, Whitman." *Diacritics* 34, no. 3/4 (2004): 31–53.

Ashton, Jennifer. *From Modernism to Postmodernism: American Poetry and Theory in the Twentieth Century*. Cambridge: Cambridge University Press, 2005.

Austin, J. L. *How to Do Things with Words*. 2nd ed. Cambridge, MA: Harvard University Press, 1975.

Bagehot, Walter. *Physics and Politics, or, Thoughts on the Application of the Principle of "Natural Selection" and "Inheritance" to Political Society*. New York: D. Appleton and Company, 1904.

Balderston, Daniel. *Out of Context: Historical Reference and the Representation of Reality in Borges*. Durham, NC: Duke University Press, 1993.

Balibar, Étienne. "Is There a 'Neo-Racism'?" Translated by Chris Turner. In *Race, Nation, Class: Ambiguous Identities*, edited by Étienne Balibar and Immanuel Wallerstein, 17–28. London: Verso, 1991.

———. "Racism as Universalism." Chap. 8 in *Masses, Classes, Ideas: Studies on Politics and Philosophy before and after Marx*, translated by James Swenson. London: Routledge, 1994.

Bastin, Georges L., Álvaro Echeverri, and Ángela Campo. "Translation and the Emancipation of Hispanic America." In *Translation, Resistance, Activism*, edited by Maria Tymoczko, 42–64. Amherst: University of Massachusetts Press, 2010.

Belnap, Jeffrey. "Headbands, Hemp Sandals, and Headdresses: The Dialectics of Dress and Self-Conception in Martí's 'Our America.'" In *José Martí's*

"Our America": From National to Hemispheric Cultural Studies, edited by Jeffrey Belnap and Raúl Fernández, 191–209. Durham, NC: Duke University Press, 1998.

Benedetti, Mario. *El ejercicio del criterio: Crítica literaria, 1950–1970.* Mexico City: Nueva Imagen, 1981.

Bernecker, Walther L., ed. *1898: Su significado para Centroamérica y el Caribe.* Madrid: Iberoamericana, 1998.

Bernstein, Richard J. "Philosophy in the Conversation of Mankind." *The Review of Metaphysics* 33, no. 4 (1980): 745–775.

Beverley, John. *Latinamericanism after 9/11.* Durham, NC: Duke University Press, 2011.

———. "The Neoconservative Turn in Latin American Literary and Cultural Criticism." *Journal of Latin American Cultural Studies* 17, no. 1 (2008): 65–83.

———. *Subalternity and Representation: Arguments in Cultural Theory.* Durham, NC: Duke University Press, 1999.

———. *Testimonio: On the Politics of Truth.* Minneapolis: University of Minnesota Press, 2004.

Billias, George Athan. *American Constitutionalism Heard Round the World, 1776–1989: A Global Perspective.* New York: New York University Press, 2009.

Blanchot, Maurice. *The Book to Come.* Translated by Charlotte Mandell. Stanford, CA: Stanford University Press, 2003.

Block de Behar, Lisa. *A Rhetoric of Silence and Other Selected Writings.* The Hague: Mouton de Gruyter, 1995.

Boghossian, Paul. *Fear of Knowledge: Against Relativism and Constructivism.* Oxford: Oxford University Press, 2006.

———. "How Are Objective Epistemic Reasons Possible?" In *Content and Justification: Philosophical Papers*, 235–266. Oxford: Oxford University Press, 2008.

Bolívar, Simón. *El Libertador: Writings of Simón Bolívar.* Edited by David Bushnell. Translated by Frederick H. Fornoff. Oxford: Oxford University Press, 2003.

Bonfil Batalla, Guillermo. *México Profundo: Reclaiming a Civilization.* Translated by Philip A. Dennis. Austin: University of Texas Press, 1996.

Borges, Jorge Luis. "Conjectural Poem." Translated by Norman Thomas di Giovanni. In *Twentieth-Century Latin American Poetry: A Bilingual Anthology*, edited by Stephen Tapscott, 145. Austin: University of Texas Press, 1996.

———. "The Detective Story." Translated by Esther Allen. In *Selected Non-Fictions*, edited by Elliot Weinberger, 491–499. New York: Penguin, 2000.

———. "Pierre Menard, Author of the *Quixote*." Translated by James E. Irby. In *Labyrinths: Selected Stories and Other Writings*, edited by Donald A. Yates and James E. Irby, 36–44. New York: New Directions, 1964.

Boullosa, Carmen. *Cielos de la tierra.* Mexico City: Alfaguara, 1997.

Brading, D. A. *The First America: The Spanish Monarchy, Creole Patriots, and the Liberal State, 1492–1867.* Cambridge: Cambridge University Press, 1991.

Brewster, Claire. *Responding to Crisis in Contemporary Mexico: The Political Writ-*

ings of Paz, Fuentes, Monsiváis, and Poniatowska. Tucson: University of Arizona Press, 2005.

Bronfman, Alejandra. *Measures of Equality: Social Science, Citizenship, and Race in Cuba, 1902–1940.* Chapel Hill: University of North Carolina Press, 2004.

Brotherston, Gordon. "*Arielismo* and Anthropophagy: *The Tempest* in Latin America." In "*The Tempest" and Its Travels,* edited by Peter Hulme and William H. Sherman, 212–219. Philadelphia: University of Pennsylvania Press, 2000.

———. "Introduction." In *Ariel,* by José Enrique Rodó, 1–19. Cambridge: Cambridge University Press, 1967.

Brown, Nicholas. "The Work of Art in the Age of Its Real Subsumption under Capital." *Nonsite.org* (2012): n.p. http://nonsite.org/editorial/the-work-of-art-in-the-age-of-its-real-subsumption-under-capital.

Bunge, Carlos Octavio. *Nuestra América: Ensayo de psicología social.* Buenos Aires: Valerio Abeledo, 1905.

Burns, Bradford. *The Poverty of Progress: Latin America in the Nineteenth Century.* Berkeley: University of California Press, 1980.

Bushnell, David. *The Making of Modern Colombia: A Nation in Spite of Itself.* Berkeley: University of California Press, 1993.

Carballo, Emmanuel, ed. *¿Qué país es éste? Los Estados Unidos y los gringos vistos por escritores mexicanos de los siglos XIX y XX.* Mexico City: Consejo Nacional para la Cultura y las Artes, 1996.

Castañón, Adolfo. *América sintaxis.* Mexico City: Siglo XXI Editores, 2009.

Castro-Gómez, Santiago. "The Missing Chapter of Empire: Postmodern Reorganization of Coloniality and Post-Fordist Capitalism." In *Globalization and the Decolonial Option,* edited by Walter D. Mignolo and Arturo Escobar, 282–302. New York: Routledge, 2010.

Central Intelligence Agency. "The World Factbook: Mexico." January 5, 2012. https://www.cia.gov/library/publications/the-world-factbook/geos/mx .html.

Cerutti Guldberg, Horacio. *Filosofía de la liberación latinoamericana.* 3rd ed. Mexico City: Fondo de Cultura Económica, 2006.

Colás, Santiago. *Postmodernity in Latin America: The Argentine Paradigm.* Durham, NC: Duke University Press, 1994.

Concha, Jaime. "Rodó's *Ariel* or Youth as *Humano Tesoro.*" In *Bridging the Atlantic: Toward a Reassessment of Iberian and Latin American Cultural Ties,* edited by Marina Pérez de Mendiola, 107–128. Albany: State University of New York Press, 1996.

Conn, Robert T. "The Pedagogic and Aesthetic States: Vitalism Revisited." Chap. 1 in *The Politics of Philology: Alfonso Reyes and the Invention of the Latin American Literary Tradition.* Lewisburg, PA: Bucknell University Press, 2002.

Conway, Christopher. "The Limits of Analogy: José Martí and the Haymarket Martyrs." *A Contracorriente: A Journal on Social History and Literature in Latin America* 2, no. 1 (2004): 33–56.

Cornejo Polar, Antonio. *Writing in the Air: Heterogeneity and the Persistence of Oral Tradition in Andean Literatures.* Translated by Lynda J. Jentsch. Durham, NC: Duke University Press, 2013.

Coronil, Fernando. *The Magical State: Nature, Money, and Modernity in Venezuela.* Chicago: University of Chicago Press, 1997.

Cortázar, Julio. *Blow-Up and Other Stories.* Translated by Paul Blackburn. New York: Random House, 1967.

Crenzel, Emilio. "Between the Voices of the State and the Human Rights Movement: *Never Again* and the Memories of the Disappeared in Argentina." *Journal of Social History* 44, no. 4 (2011): 1063–1076.

Danto, Arthur. *The Transfiguration of the Commonplace: A Philosophy of Art.* Cambridge, MA: Harvard University Press, 1981.

Darío, Rubén. "El triunfo de Calibán." Edited by Carlos Jáuregui. *Revista Iberoamericana* 64, nos. 184–185 (1998): 451–456.

Davidson, Donald. "Objectivity and Practical Reason." In *Reasoning Practically,* edited by Edna Ullman-Margalit, 17–26. Oxford: Oxford University Press, 2000.

———. "Truth Rehabilitated." In *Rorty and His Critics,* edited by Robert B. Brandom, 65–74. Oxford: Blackwell, 2000.

de la Campa, Román. *Latin Americanism.* Minneapolis: University of Minnesota Press, 1999.

de la Fuente, Alejandro. *A Nation for All: Race, Inequality, and Politics in Twentieth-Century Cuba.* Chapel Hill: University of North Carolina Press, 2001.

de Man, Paul. "Autobiography as De-facement." *MLN* 94, no. 5 (1979): 919–930.

Derrida, Jacques. *The Ear of the Other: Otobiography, Transference, Translation.* Edited by Christie McDonald. Translated by Peggy Kamuf. Lincoln: University of Nebraska Press, 1985.

Di Stefano, Eugenio. "From Shopping Malls to Memory Museums: Reconciling the Recent Past in the Uruguayan Neoliberal State." *Dissidences* 4, no. 8 (2012): n.p. http://digitalcommons.bowdoin.edu/dissidences/vol4/iss8/8.

Di Stefano, Eugenio, and Emilio Sauri. "Making It Visible: Latin Americanist Criticism, Literature, and the Question of Exploitation Today." *Nonsite .org* (2014): n.p. http://nonsite.org/article/making-it-visible.

Dove, Patrick. *The Catastrophe of Modernity: Tragedy and the Nation in Latin American Literature.* Lewisburg, PA: Bucknell University Press, 2004.

Draper, Susana. *Afterlives of Confinement: Spatial Transitions in Postdictatorship Latin America.* Pittsburgh, PA: University of Pittsburgh Press, 2012.

Dröscher, Barbara, and Carlos Rincón, eds. *Acercamientos a Carmen Boullosa: Actas del simposio "Conjugarse en infinitivo en la escritoria Carmen Boullosa."* Berlin: Verlag Walter Frey, 1999.

Dussel, Enrique. "Philosophy in Latin America in the Twentieth Century:

Problems and Currents." In *Latin American Philosophy: Currents, Issues, Debates*, edited by Eduardo Mendieta, 11–53. Bloomington: Indiana University Press, 2003.

Dussel Peters, Enrique. *Polarizing Mexico: The Impact of Liberalization Strategy*. Boulder, CO: Lynne Rienner, 2000.

Echeverría, Esteban. *Obras escogidas*. Edited by Beatriz Sarlo and Carlos Altamirano. Caracas: Biblioteca Ayacucho, 1991.

Estrada, Oswaldo. "(Re)Constructions of Memory and Identity Formation in Carmen Boullosa's Postcolonial Writings." *South Atlantic Review* 74, no. 4 (2009): 131–148.

Fernández Retamar, Roberto. "América Latina y el trasfondo de occidente." In *América Latina en sus ideas*, edited by Leopoldo Zea, 300–330. Mexico City: Siglo XXI Editores, 1986.

———. *Caliban and Other Essays*. Translated by Edward Baker. Minneapolis: University of Minnesota Press, 1989.

———. *Para una teoría de la literatura hispanoamericana*. Bogotá: Publicaciones del Instituto Caro y Cuervo, 1995.

Ferrer, Ada. *Insurgent Cuba: Race, Nation, and Revolution, 1868–1898*. Chapel Hill: University of North Carolina Press, 1999.

———. "The Silence of Patriots: Race and Nationalism in Martí's Cuba." In *José Martí's "Our America": From National to Hemispheric Cultural Studies*, edited by Jeffrey Belnap and Raúl Fernandez, 228–249. Durham, NC: Duke University Press, 1998.

Fields, Karen E., and Barbara J. Fields. *Racecraft: The Soul of Inequality in American Life*. London: Verso, 2012.

Fish, Stanley. *Doing What Comes Naturally: Change, Rhetoric, and the Practice of Theory in Literary and Legal Studies*. Durham, NC: Duke University Press, 1989.

———. "Liberalism Doesn't Exist." Chap. 10 in *There's No Such Thing as Free Speech, and It's a Good Thing, Too*. Oxford: Oxford University Press, 1994.

———. "A Reply to J. Judd Owen." *American Political Science Review* 93, no. 4 (1999): 925–930.

———. *The Trouble with Principle*. Cambridge, MA: Harvard University Press, 1999.

Foley, Richard. *When Is True Belief Knowledge?* Princeton, NJ: Princeton University Press, 2012.

Forjas, Camilla. *Cosmopolitanism in the Americas*. West Lafayette, IN: Purdue University Press, 2005.

Fornet-Betancourt, Raúl. *Estudios de filosofía latinoamericana*. Mexico City: Universidad Nacional Autónoma de México, 1992.

Fouillée, Alfred. *L'idée moderne du droit en Allemagne, en Angleterre et en France*. Paris: Librarie Hachette, 1878. Partial English-language translation by Mrs. Franklin W. Scott and Joseph P. Chamberlain in *Modern French Legal Philosophy*, by Alfred Fouillée, Joseph Charmont, Léon Duguit, and René Demogue, 1-62 ("General Characteristics of French Legal Thought"), 149-234 ("Synthesis of Idealism and Naturalism"). New York: Macmillan, 1921.

——. *Le mouvement idéaliste et la reactión contre la science positive*. Paris: Félix Alcan, 1896.

Fountain, Anne. "Martí and Race: An Overview." Chap. 2 in *José Martí, the United States, and Race*. Gainesville: University Press of Florida, 2014.

Franco, Jean. *Cruel Modernity*. Durham, NC: Duke University Press, 2013.

——. *The Decline and Fall of the Lettered City: Latin America in the Cold War*. Cambridge, MA: Harvard University Press, 2002.

——. *Spanish American Literature since Independence*. London: Ernest Benn, 1973.

Fraser, Nancy. *Justice Interruptus: Critical Reflections on the "Postsocialist" Condition*. London: Routledge, 1997.

Fried, Michael. "Art and Objecthood." In *Art and Objecthood: Essays and Reviews*, 148–172. Chicago: University of Chicago Press, 1998.

Galeano, Eduardo. *Genesis*. Vol. 1 of *Memory of Fire*. Translated by Cedric Belfrage. New York: W. W. Norton, 1998.

Gallardo, Helio. "El pensar en América Latina; Introducción al problema de la conformación de nuestra conciencia: A. Salazar Bondy y L. Zea." *Revista de Filosofía de la Universidad de Costa Rica* 12, no. 35 (1974): 183–210.

Gamio, Manuel. *Forjando patria: Pro-nacionalismo*. Translated by Fernando Armstrong-Fumero. Boulder: University Press of Colorado, 2010.

García Calderón, Francisco. *La creación de un continente*. Paris: Librería Ollendorf, 1912.

García Canclini, Néstor. *Consumers and Citizens: Globalization and Multicultural Conflicts*. Translated by George Yúdice. Minneapolis: University of Minnesota Press, 2001.

——. "North Americans or Latin Americans? The Redefinition of Mexican Identity and the Free Trade Agreements." In *Mass Media and Free Trade: NAFTA and the Cultural Industries*, edited by Emile G. McAnany and Kenton T. Wilkinson, 142–156. Austin: University of Texas Press, 1996.

García Morales, Alfonso. "Ariel en México." In *El ateneo de México (1906–1914): Orígenes de la cultura mexicana contemporánea*, 119–132. Seville: Consejo Superior de Investigación Científica, Escuela de Estudios Hispano-Americanos, 1992.

Genette, Gérard. *Palimpsests: Literature in the Second Degree*. Translated by Channa Newman and Claude Doubinsky. Lincoln: University of Nebraska Press, 1997.

Gerbi, Antonello. "The Reaction to de Pauw in Spanish America." Chap. 6 in *The Dispute of the New World: The History of a Polemic, 1750–1900*, translated by Jeremy Moyle. Pittsburgh, PA: University of Pittsburgh Press, 1973.

Gillman, Susan. "Otra vez Caliban / Encore Caliban: Adaptation, Translation, Americas Studies." *American Literary History* 20, nos. 1–2 (2008): 187–209.

González Echevarría, Roberto. "A Brief History of Spanish American Literature." In *The Cambridge History of Latin American Literature*, vol. 1, *Discovery to Modernism*, edited by Roberto González Echevarría and Enrique Pupo-Walker, 7–32. Cambridge: Cambridge University Press, 1996.

———. "The Case of the Speaking Statue: *Ariel* and the Magisterial Rhetoric of the Latin American Essay." Chap. 1 in *The Voice of the Masters: Writing and Authority in Modern Latin American Literature*. Austin: University of Texas Press, 1985.

Graff Zivin, Erin. *Figurative Inquisitions: Torture and Truth in the Luso-Hispanic Atlantic*. Evanston, IL: Northwestern University Press, 2014.

———. "Introduction: Reading Otherwise." In *The Ethics of Latin American Literary Criticism: Reading Otherwise*, edited by Erin Graff Zivin, 1–7. New York: Palgrave Macmillan, 2007.

Gran, Peter. *The Rise of the Rich: A New View of Modern World History*. Syracuse, NY: Syracuse University Press, 2009.

Grases, Pedro. "Traducciones de interés político-cultural en la época de la independencia de Venezuela." In *Escritos selectos*, edited by Arturo Uslar Pietri, 108–118. Caracas: Biblioteca Ayacucho, 1989.

Groff, Ruth. *Critical Realism, Post-Positivism and the Possibility of Knowledge*. London: Routledge, 2004.

Guerra, Lillian. *The Myth of José Martí: Conflicting Nationalisms in Early Twentieth-Century Cuba*. Chapel Hill: University of North Carolina Press, 2005.

Guillén, Nicolás. *Obra poética*, 2 vols. Havana: Instituto Cubano del Libro, 1972.

Haack, Susan. *Evidence and Inquiry: A Pragmatist Reconstruction of Epistemology*. Amherst, NY: Prometheus Books, 2009.

Hale, Charles A. *Mexican Liberalism in the Age of Mora*. New Haven, CT: Yale University Press, 1968.

———. "Political Ideas and Ideologies in Latin America, 1870–1930." In *Ideas and Ideologies in Twentieth-Century Latin America*, edited by Leslie Bethell, 133–205. Cambridge: Cambridge University Press, 1996.

Hale, Charles R. "Does Multiculturalism Menace? Governance, Cultural Rights and the Politics of Identity in Guatemala." *Journal of Latin American Studies* 34 (August 2002): 485–524.

Harvey, David. *A Brief History of Neoliberalism*. Oxford: Oxford University Press, 2005.

Hayles, N. Katherine. "Translating Media: Why We Should Rethink Textuality." *Yale Journal of Criticism* 16, no. 2 (2003): 263–290.

Healy, David. *James G. Blaine and Latin America*. Columbia: University of Missouri Press, 2001.

Helg, Aline. *Our Rightful Share: The Afro-Cuban Struggle for Equality, 1886–1912*. Chapel Hill: University of North Carolina Press, 1995.

———. "Race in Argentina and Cuba, 1880–1930." In *The Idea of Race in Latin America, 1870–1940*, edited by Richard Graham, 37–69. Austin: University of Texas Press, 1990.

Henríquez Ureña, Pedro. *Las corrientes literarias en la América Hispánica*. Mexico City: Fondo de Cultura Económica, 1954.

———. *Seis ensayos en búsca de nuestra expresión*. In *Obra crítica de Pedro Henríquez Ureña*, edited by Emma Susana Speratti Piñero, 241–330. Mexico City: Fondo de Cultura Económica, 1960.

Hind, Emily. "Historical Arguments: Carlos Salinas and Mexican Women Writers." *Discourse* 23, no. 2 (2001): 82–101.

Hiraldo, Carlos. *Segregated Miscegenation: On the Treatment of Racial Hybridity in the U.S. and Latin American Literary Traditions*. London: Routledge, 2003.

Horowitz, Donald L. "*The Federalist* Abroad in the World." In *The Federalist Papers*, edited by Ian Shapiro, 502–532. New Haven, CT: Yale University Press, 2009.

Hutcheon, Linda. *A Poetics of Postmodernism: History, Theory, Fiction*. London: Routledge, 1988.

Jackson, Richard L. *Black Literature and Humanism in Latin America*. Athens: University of Georgia Press, 1988.

Jáuregui, Carlos. "Calibán, ícono del 98. A propósito de un artículo de Rubén Darío." *Revista Iberoamericana* 64, nos. 184–185 (1998): 441–449.

Jauss, Hans Robert. "The Theory of Reception: A Retrospective of Its Unrecognized Prehistory." In *Literary Theory Today*, edited by Peter Collier and Helga Geyer-Ryan, 53–73. Ithaca, NY: Cornell University Press, 1990.

Jenkins, Keith. *Rethinking History*. London: Routledge, 2003.

Johnson, David E. *Kant's Dog: On Borges, Philosophy, and the Time of Translation*. Albany: State University of New York Press, 2012.

Jörgensen, Beth E. *The Writings of Elena Poniatowska: Engaging Dialogues*. Austin: University of Texas Press, 1994.

Jrade, Cathy L. *Modernismo, Modernity, and the Development of Spanish American Literature*. Austin: University of Texas Press, 1998.

Kalimán, Ricardo J. "Sobre la construcción del objeto en la crítica literaria latinoamericana." *Revista de Crítica Literaria Latinoamericana* 37 (1993): 307–317.

Kinsbruner, Jay. *Independence in Spanish America: Civil Wars, Revolutions, and Underdevelopment*. Albuquerque: University of New Mexico Press, 1994.

Klein, Kerwin. "On the Emergence of *Memory* in Historical Discourse." *Representations* 69 (2000): 127–150.

Kloppenberg, James T. "The Philosophy of the *Via Media*." Chap. 1 in *Social Democracy and Progressivism in European and American Thought, 1870–1920*. Oxford: Oxford University Press, 1986.

Klor de Alva, J. Jorge. "Colonialism and Postcolonialism as (Latin) American Mirages." *Colonial Latin American Review* 1, nos. 1–2 (1992): 3–23.

Knapp, Steven, and Walter Benn Michaels. "Against Theory." *Critical Inquiry* 8 (1982): 723–742.

———. "Not a Matter of Interpretation." *San Diego Law Review* 42, no. 2 (2005): 651–668.

Kovic, Christine. *Mayan Voices for Human Rights: Displaced Catholics in Highland Chiapas.* Austin: University of Texas Press, 2005.

Kozlarek, Oliver, ed. *Entre cosmopolitismo y "conciencia del mundo."* Mexico City: Siglo XXI Editores, 2007.

Kuper, Adam. *Culture: The Anthropologists' Account.* Cambridge, MA: Harvard University Press, 1999.

Kusch, Rodolfo. *Indigenous and Popular Thinking in América.* Translated by María Lugones and Joshua M. Price. Durham, NC: Duke University Press, 2010.

Laclau, Ernesto. "Structure, History and the Political." In *Contingency, Hegemony, Universality: Contemporary Dialogues on the Left,* edited by Judith Butler, Ernesto Laclau, and Slavoj Žižek, 182–212. London: Verso, 2000.

———. "Universalism, Particularism, and the Question of Identity." *October* 61 (1992): 83–90.

Lagmanovich, David. "Lectura de un ensayo: 'Nuestra América' de José Martí." In *Nuevos asedios al modernismo,* edited by Ivan A. Schulman, 235–245. Madrid: Taurus, 1987.

Langley, Lester D. *The Americas in the Age of Revolution, 1750–1850.* New Haven, CT: Yale University Press, 1996.

Larrain, Jorge. *Identity and Modernity in Latin America.* Cambridge: Polity Press, 2000.

Leal, Luis. *A Luis Leal Reader.* Edited by Ilan Stavans. Evanston, IL: Northwestern University Press, 2007.

Levinson, Brett. *The Ends of Literature: The Latin American "Boom" in the Neoliberal Marketplace.* Stanford, CA: Stanford University Press, 2001.

Lipp, Solomon. *U.S.A.–Spanish America: Challenge and Response.* London: Tamesis Books, 1994.

Lomas, Laura. *Translating Empire: José Martí, Migrant Latino Subjects, and American Modernities.* Durham, NC: Duke University Press, 2008.

Lomnitz-Adler, Claudio. *Deep Mexico, Silent Mexico: An Anthropology of Nationalism.* Minneapolis: University of Minnesota Press, 2001.

López, Alfred J. *José Martí and the Future of Cuban Nationalisms.* Gainesville: University Press of Florida, 2006.

López-Lozano, Miguel. "The Dream of Mestizo Mexico: Memory and History in Carmen Boullosa's *Cielos de la tierra.*" Chap. 3 in *Utopian Dreams, Apocalyptic Nightmares: Globalization in Recent Mexican and Chicano Narrative.* West Lafayette, IN: Purdue University Press, 2008.

Lorenzano, Sandra. "Angels among Ruins." In *Telling Ruins in Latin America,* edited by Michael J. Lazzara and Vicky Unruh, 249–260. New York: Palgrave, 2009.

Loss, Jacqueline. *Cosmopolitanisms and Latin America: Against the Destiny of Place.* New York: Palgrave Macmillan, 2005.

Loveman, Brian. *No Higher Law: American Foreign Policy and the Western Hemisphere since 1776.* Chapel Hill: University of North Carolina Press, 2010.

Lund, Joshua. *The Impure Imagination: Toward a Critical Hybridity in Latin American Writing.* Minneapolis: University of Minnesota Press, 2006.

Lynch, John. "The Origins of Spanish American Independence." In *The Cambridge History of Latin America*, vol. 3, *From Independence to c. 1870,* edited by Leslie Bethell, 3–48. Cambridge: Cambridge University Press, 1987.

Macklin, Ruth. *Against Relativism: Cultural Diversity and the Search for Ethical Universals.* Oxford: Oxford University Press, 1999.

MacLeod, Dag. *Downsizing the State: Privatization and the Limits of Neoliberal Reform in Mexico.* University Park: Pennsylvania State University Press, 2004.

Mariátegui, José Carlos. *Seven Interpretive Essays on Peruvian Reality.* Translated by Marjory Urquidi. Austin: University of Texas Press, 1971.

Marinello, Juan. *Obras martianas.* Edited by Ramón Losada Aldana. Caracas: Biblioteca Ayacucho, 1987.

Martí, José. *Obras completas.* 27 vols. Havana: Editorial Nacional de Cuba, 1963.

———. *Selected Writings.* Translated by Esther Allen. New York: Penguin, 2002.

———. *Versos sencillos / Simple Verses.* Translated by Manuel A. Tellechea. Houston: Arte Público Press, 1997.

Martínez-Echazábal, Lourdes. "Martí and Race: A Re-evaluation." In *Re-reading José Martí,* edited by Julio Rodríguez-Luis, 115–126. Albany: State University of New York Press, 1999.

Martínez Novo, Carmen. *Who Defines Indigenous? Identities, Development, Intellectuals, and the State in Northern Mexico.* New Brunswick, NJ: Rutgers University Press, 2005.

Masiello, Francine. *The Art of Transition: Latin American Culture and Neoliberal Crisis.* Durham, NC: Duke University Press, 2001.

Mazzei, Julie. *Death Squads or Self-Defense Forces? How Paramilitary Groups Emerge and Threaten Democracy in Latin America.* Chapel Hill: University of North Carolina Press, 2009.

McGann, Jerome. *The Textual Condition.* Princeton, NJ: Princeton University Press, 1991.

McPherson, Alan. "*Antiyanquismo*: Nascent Scholarship, Ancient Sentiments." In *Anti-Americanism in Latin America and the Caribbean,* edited by Alan McPherson, 1–36. New York: Berghahn Books, 2006.

———. *Yankee No! Anti-Americanism in U.S.–Latin American Relations.* Cambridge, MA: Harvard University Press, 2003.

Mejías-López, Alejandro. *The Inverted Conquest: The Myth of Modernity and the Transatlantic Onset of Modernism.* Nashville, TN: Vanderbilt University Press, 2009.

Mendieta, Eduardo. "The Ethics of (Not) Knowing: Take Care of Ethics and Knowledge Will Come of Its Own Accord." In *Decolonizing Epistemologies: Latina/o Theology and Philosophy,* edited by Ada María Isasi-Díaz and Eduardo Mendieta, 247–264. New York: Fordham University Press, 2012.

Menton, Seymour. *Latin America's New Historical Novel.* Austin: University of Texas Press, 1993.

Michaels, Walter Benn. *Our America: Nativism, Modernism, and Pluralism.* Durham, NC: Duke University Press, 1995.

———. "Race into Culture: A Critical Genealogy of Cultural Identity." *Critical Inquiry* 18, no. 4 (1992): 655–685.

———. *The Shape of the Signifier: 1967 to the End of History.* Princeton, NJ: Princeton University Press, 2004.

———. *The Trouble with Diversity: How We Learned to Love Identity and Ignore Inequality.* New York: Metropolitan Books, 2006.

Mignolo, Walter. "Afterword: Human Understanding and (Latin) American Interests—The Politics and Sensibilities of Geocultural Locations." *Poetics Today* 16, no. 1 (1995): 171–214.

———. *The Darker Side of the Renaissance: Literacy, Territoriality, and Colonization.* Ann Arbor: University of Michigan Press, 1995.

———. *The Darker Side of Western Modernity: Global Futures, Decolonial Options.* Durham, NC: Duke University Press, 2011.

———. *Global Histories/Local Designs: Coloniality, Subaltern Knowledges, and Border Thinking.* Princeton, NJ: Princeton University Press, 2000.

———. "Introduction: Immigrant Consciousness." In *Indigenous and Popular Thinking in América*, by Rodolfo Kusch, xiii–liv. Durham, NC: Duke University Press, 2010.

———. "Occidentalización, imperialismo, globalización: Herencias coloniales y teorías postcoloniales." In *Theoretical Debates in Spanish American Literature: The Professoriate in Crisis*, edited by David William Foster and Daniel Altamiranda, 69–82. New York: Garland, 1997.

———. "Posoccidentalismo: Las epistemologías fronterizas y el dilema de los estudios (latinoamericanos) de area." *Revista Iberoamericana* 62, nos. 176–177 (1996): 679–696.

Miller, Nicola. *Reinventing Modernity in Latin America: Intellectuals Imagine the Future, 1900–1930.* New York: Palgrave Macmillan, 2008.

Miranda, Francisco de. *Archivo del general Miranda.* Vol. 15. Caracas: Academia Nacional de Historia, 1929.

Miró Quesada, Francisco. *Despertar y proyecto de filosofar latinoamericano.* Mexico City: Fondo de Cultura Económica, 1974.

Mitchell, W. J. T., ed. *Against Theory: Literary Studies and the New Pragmatism.* Chicago: University of Chicago Press, 1982.

Molloy, Sylvia. "The Politics of Posing: Translating Decadence in Fin-de-Siècle Latin America." In *Perennial Decay: On the Aesthetics and Politics of Decadence*, edited by Liz Constable, Dennis Denisoff, and Matthew Potolsky, 183–197. Philadelphia: University of Pennsylvania Press, 1999.

———. *Signs of Borges.* Translated by Oscar Montero. Durham, NC: Duke University Press, 1994.

Morán, Francisco. *Martí, la justicia infinita: Notas sobre ética y otredad en la escritura martiana*. Madrid: Editorial Verbum, 2014.

Moraña, Mabel. "The Boom of the Subaltern." In *The Latin American Cultural Studies Reader*, edited by Ana Del Sarto, Alicia Ríos, and Abril Trigo, 643–654. Durham, NC: Duke University Press, 2004.

Moreiras, Alberto. *The Exhaustion of Difference: The Politics of Latin American Cultural Studies*. Durham, NC: Duke University Press, 2001.

———. *Tercer espacio: Literatura y duelo en América Latina*. Santiago: LOM Ediciones/Universidad Arcis, 1999.

Morris, Stephen D. "Between Neo-liberalism and Neo-indigenismo: Reconstructing National Identity in Mexico." *National Identities* 3, no. 3 (2001): 239–255.

Nariño, Antonio. *El Precursor: Documentos sobre la vida pública y privada del general Antonio Nariño*. Vol. 2 of *Biblioteca de historia nacional*. Edited by Eduardo Posada and Pedro M. Ibáñez. Bogotá: Imprenta Nacional, 1903.

Newcomb, Robert Patrick. "José Enrique Rodó: Iberoamérica, the *Magna Patria*, and the Question of Brazil." Chap. 3 in *Nossa and Nuestra América: Inter-American Dialogues*. West Lafayette, IN: Purdue University Press, 2012.

Nuccetelli, Susana. *Latin American Thought: Philosophical Problems and Arguments*. Boulder, CO: Westview Press, 2002.

Olick, Jeffrey K., Vered Vinitzky-Seroussi, and Daniel Levy. Introduction to *The Collective Memory Reader*, edited by Jeffrey K. Olick, Vered Vinitzky-Seroussi, and Daniel Levy, 3–62. Oxford: Oxford University Press, 2011.

Onís, José de. *The United States as Seen by Spanish American Writers (1776–1890)*. New York: Hispanic Institute of the United States, 1952.

Ortega, Julio. *Poetics of Change: The New Spanish American Narrative*. Translated by Galen D. Greaser in collaboration with the author. Austin: University of Texas Press, 1984.

Ortiz, Fernando. "Martí and the Race Problem." *Phylon* 3, no. 3 (1942), 264.

Otero, Gerardo. "Neoliberal Reform and Politics in Mexico." In *Neoliberalism Revisited: Economic Restructuring and Mexico's Political Future*, edited by Gerardo Otero, 1–26. Boulder, CO: Westview Press, 1996.

Palermo, Zulma. "De apropiaciones y desplazamientos: El proyecto teórico de Fernández Retamar." In *Roberto Fernández Retamar y los estudios latinoamericanos*, edited by Elzbieta Sklodowska and Ben A. Heller, 181–198. Pittsburgh, PA: Instituto Internacional de Literatura Iberoamericana, 2000.

Paz, Octavio. *The Bow and the Lyre*. Translated by Ruth L. C. Simms. 2nd ed. Austin: University of Texas Press, 1987.

———. "Mexico and the United States." Translated by Rachel Phillips Belash. In *The Labyrinth of Solitude, the Other Mexico, and Other Essays*, 355–376. New York: Grove, 1985.

———. "Poesía en movimiento." In *Poesía en movimiento: México, 1915–1966*, edited by Octavio Paz, Alí Chumacero, José Emilio Pacheco, and Homero Aridjis, 3–34. Mexico City: Siglo XXI Editores, 1979.

———. "Poesía mexicana moderna." In *Obras completas*, vol. 4, *Generaciones y semblanzas: Dominio mexicano*, 60–68. Mexico City: Fondo de Cultura Económica, 1994.

Peirce, Charles S. *Philosophical Writings of Peirce*. Edited by Justus Buchler. Mineola, NY: Dover, 1955.

Pereda, Clemente. *Rodó's Main Sources*. San Juan: Imprenta Venezuela, 1948.

Pérez, Diana I. "The Ontology of Art: What Can We Learn from Borges's 'Menard?'" *New Centennial Review* 11, no. 1 (2011): 75–89.

Pérez, Louis A. *Cuba: Between Reform and Revolution*. Oxford: Oxford University Press, 1995.

Poey Baró, Dionisio. "'Race' and Anti-Racism in José Martí's 'Mi Raza.'" *Contributions in Black Studies* 12 (1994): 55–61.

Portuondo, José Antonio. *Crítica de la época y otros ensayos*. Santa Clara: Universidad Central de las Villas, 1965.

Quijano, Aníbal. "Modernity, Identity, and Utopia in Latin America." *Boundary 2* 20, no. 3 (1993): 140–155.

Rabasa, José. *Without History: Subaltern Studies, the Zapatista Insurgency, and the Specter of History*. Pittsburgh, PA: University of Pittsburgh Press, 2010.

Rachels, James. "The Challenge of Cultural Relativism." In *Ethics: Essential Readings in Moral Theory*, edited by George Sher, 151–158. London: Routledge, 2012.

Racine, Karen. "Finding the Founding Fathers: Miranda's Tour of the United States (1783–84)." Chap. 2 in *Francisco de Miranda: A Transatlantic Life in the Age of Revolution*. Wilmington, DE: SR Books, 2003.

Rama, Ángel. *The Lettered City*. Edited and translated by John Charles Chasteen. Durham, NC: Duke University Press, 1996.

Ramos, Jorge Abelardo. *Historia de la nación latinoamericana*. Buenos Aires: A. Peña Lillo, 1973.

Ramos, Julio. *Divergent Modernities: Culture and Politics in Nineteenth-Century Latin America*. Translated by John D. Blanco. Durham, NC: Duke University Press, 2001.

———. "Hemispheric Domains: 1891 and the Origins of Latin Americanism." *Journal of Latin American Cultural Studies* 10, no. 3 (2001): 237–251.

Rancière, Jacques. *Disagreement: Politics and Philosophy*. Translated by Julie Rose. Minneapolis: University of Minnesota Press, 1999.

Rangel, Carlos. *The Latin Americans: Their Love-Hate Relationship with the United States*. New Brunswick, NJ: Transaction Books, 1987.

Real de Azúa, Carlos. "Prólogo a *Ariel*." In *Ariel: Motivos de Proteo*, edited by Ángel Rama, ix–xxxi. Caracas: Biblioteca Ayacucho, 1976.

Reid, Anna. "Disintegration, Dismemberment and Discovery of Identities and Histories: Searching the 'Gaps' for Depositories of Alternative Memory in the Narratives of Diamela Eltit and Carmen Boullosa." *Bulletin of Latin American Research* 17, no. 1 (1998): 81–92.

Reid, John T. "The Rise and Decline of the Ariel-Caliban Antithesis in Spanish America." *The Americas* 34, no. 3 (1978): 345–355.

Rodó, José Enrique. *Ariel*. Translated by Margaret Sayers Peden. Austin: University of Texas Press, 1988.

———. *El mirador de Próspero*. Montevideo: C. García y Cía., 1939.

———. *Rubén Darío: Su personalidad literaria, su última obra*. Montevideo: Dornaleche y Reyes, 1899.

Rodríguez, Jeanette, and Ted Fortier. *Cultural Memory: Resistance, Faith, and Identity*. Austin: University of Texas Press, 2007.

Rodríguez-Luis, Julio. "Introduction: On the Re-evaluation of Martí." In *Rereading José Martí: One Hundred Years Later*, edited by Julio Rodríguez-Luis. Albany: State University of New York Press, 1999.

Rodríguez Monegal, Emir. "Borges and Derrida: Apothecaries." In *Borges and His Successors: The Borgesian Impact on Literature and the Arts*, edited by Edna Aizenberg, 128–138. Columbia: University of Missouri Press, 1990.

———. "La metamorfosis de Calibán." In *Obra selecta*, edited by Lisa Block de Behar, 172–180. Caracas: Biblioteca Ayacucho, 2003.

Rodríguez O., Jaime E. *The Independence of Spanish America*. Cambridge: Cambridge University Press, 1998.

Roig, Arturo Andrés. *Teoría y crítica del pensamiento latinoamericano*. Mexico City: Fondo de Cultura Económica, 1981.

Rojas, Rafael. "The Moral Frontier: Cuba, 1898. Discourses at War." Translated by Licia Fiol-Matta. *Social Text* no. 59 (1999): 145–160.

———. "'Otro gallo cantaría': Essay on the First Cuban Republicanism." In *The Cuban Republic and José Martí: Reception and Use of a National Symbol*, edited by Mauricio A. Font and Alfonso W. Quiroz, 7–17. Lanham, MD: Lexington Books, 2006.

Rojas Mix, Miguel. "Bilbao y el hallazgo de América Latina: Unión continental, socialista y libertaria." *Cahiers du Monde Hispanique et Luso-brésilien* 46 (1986): 35–47.

———. "Raza y 'pueblo enfermo.'" In *Los cien nombres de América: Eso que descubrió Colón*. San José: Editorial de la Universidad de Costa Rica, 1997.

Rorty, Richard. *Philosophy and the Mirror of Nature*. Princeton, NJ: Princeton University Press, 2009.

Sacerío-Gari, Enrique. "Towards Pierre Menard." *MLN* 95, no. 2 (1980): 460–471.

Saer, Juan José. *The Witness*. Translated by Margaret Jull Costa. London: Serpent's Tail, 1990.

Salazar Bondy, Augusto. *¿Existe una filosofía de nuestra América?* 12th ed. Mexico City: Siglo XXI Editores, 1988.

Saldívar, José David. *The Dialectics of Our America: Genealogy, Cultural Critique, and Literary History*. Durham, NC: Duke University Press, 1991.

Salles, Arleen. "Rodó, Race, and Morality." In *Forging People: Race, Ethnicity, and Nationality in Hispanic American and Latino/a Thought*, edited by Jorge J. E. Gracia, 181–202. Notre Dame, IN: University of Notre Dame Press, 2011.

Salomon, Noël. "José Martí y la toma de conciencia latinoamericana." In *Lectura crítica de la literatura latinoamericana*, vol. 2, *La formación de las culturas nacionales*, edited by Saúl Sosnowski, 223–238. Caracas: Biblioteca Ayacucho, 1996.

Sánchez, Luis Alberto. *Balance y liquidación del novecientos: Tuvimos maestros en nuestra América?* Lima: Universidad Nacional Mayor de San Marcos, 1968.

Santí, Enrico Mario. "'Our America,' the Gilded Age, and the Crisis of Latinamericanism." In *José Martí's "Our America": From National to Hemispheric Cultural Studies*, edited by Jeffrey Belnap and Raúl Fernández, 179–190. Durham, NC: Duke University Press, 1998.

Sarlo, Beatriz. *Jorge Luis Borges: A Writer on the Edge*. Edited by John King. London: Verso, 1993.

———. *Tiempo pasado: Cultura de la memoria y giro subjetivo*. Mexico City: Siglo XXI Editores, 2006.

Sarmiento, Domingo Faustino. "Conflictos y armonías de las razas en América." In *Pensamiento positivista latinoamericano*, vol. 1, edited by Leopoldo Zea, 68–78. Caracas: Biblioteca Ayacucho, 1980.

———. *Facundo: Civilization and Barbarism*. Translated by Kathleen Ross. Berkeley: University of California Press, 2003.

Sauri, Emilio. "'A la pinche modernidad': Literary Form and the End of History in Roberto Bolaño's *Los detectives salvajes*." *MLN* 125, no. 2 (2010): 406–432.

Schulman, Ivan A. "Introduction." In *The Autobiography of a Slave*, by Juan Francisco Manzano, translated by Evelyn Picon Garfield. Detroit: Wayne State University Press, 1996.

———. *El proyecto inconcluso: La vigencia del modernismo*. Mexico City: Siglo XXI Editores, 2002.

Schutte, Ofelia. *Cultural Identity and Social Liberation in Latin American Thought*. Albany: State University of New York Press, 1993.

Simmons, Merle E. *Los escritos de Juan Pablo Viscardo y Guzmán: Precursor de la independencia hispanoamericana*. Caracas: Universidad Católica Andrés Bello, 1983.

Siraganian, Lisa. *Modernism's Other Work: The Art Object's Political Life*. Oxford: Oxford University Press, 2012.

Siskind, Mariano. *Cosmopolitan Desires: Global Modernity and World Literature in Latin America*. Evanston, IL: Northwestern University Press, 2014.

Snyder, Louis L. "The Idea of Racialism: Its Meaning and History." In *Racism: Essential Readings*, edited by Ellis Cashmore and James Jennings, 91–97. London: Sage, 2001.

Sobrevilla, David. "El surgimiento de la idea de Nuestra América en los ensayistas latinoamericanos decimonónicos." *Revista de Crítica Literaria Latinoamericana* 50 (1999): 147–163.

Soler, Ricaurte. *Idea y cuestión nacional latinoamericanas: De la independencia a la emergencia del imperialismo.* Mexico City: Siglo XXI Editores, 1987.

Sommer, Doris. *Proceed with Caution, When Engaged by Minority Writing in the Americas.* Cambridge, MA: Harvard University Press, 1999.

Sorensen Goodrich, Diana. *Facundo and the Construction of Argentine Culture.* Austin: University of Texas Press, 1996.

———. *The Reader and the Text: Interpretative Strategies for Latin American Literatures.* Purdue University Monographs in Romance Languages 18. Amsterdam: John Benjamins, 1985.

Stabb, Martin S. "The Sick Continent and Its Diagnosticians." Chap. 2 of *The Dissenting Voice: The New Essay of Spanish America, 1960–1985.* Austin: University of Texas Press, 1994.

———. *In Quest of Identity: Patterns in the Spanish American Essay of Ideas, 1890–1960.* Chapel Hill: University of North Carolina Press, 1967.

———. "Martí and the Racists." *Hispania* 40, no. 4 (1957): 434–439.

Staum, Martin S. "Heredity and Milieu in the *Revue philosophique.*" Chap. 5 in *Nature and Nurture in French Social Sciences, 1859–1914 and Beyond.* Montreal and Kingston: McGill-Queen's University Press, 2011.

Steger, Manfred B., and Ravi K. Roy. *Neoliberalism: A Very Short Introduction.* Oxford: Oxford University Press, 2010.

Steiner, George. *After Babel: Aspects of Language and Translation.* Oxford: Oxford University Press, 1992.

Stepan, Nancy Leys. *The Hour of Eugenics: Race, Gender, and Nation in Latin America.* Ithaca, NY: Cornell University Press, 1991.

Stoetzer, O. Carlos. *The Scholastic Roots of the Spanish American Revolution.* New York: Fordham University Press, 1979.

Sutcliffe, Bob. "World Inequality and Globalization." *Oxford Review of Economic Policy* 20, no. 1 (2004): 15–37.

Taylor, Diana. *The Archive and the Repertoire: Performing Cultural Memory in the Americas.* Durham, NC: Duke University Press, 2003.

Taylor, Paul C. *Race: A Philosophical Introduction.* Cambridge: Polity, 2004.

Thomas, Hugh. *Cuba: The Pursuit of Freedom.* New York: Harper, 1971.

Trigg, Roger. *Reason and Commitment.* Cambridge: Cambridge University Press, 1973.

Van Cott, Donna Lee. "Constitutional Reform in the Andes: Redefining Indigenous-State Relations." In *Multiculturalism in Latin America: Indigenous Rights, Diversity and Democracy,* edited by Rachel Sieder, 45–73. London: Palgrave Macmillan, 2002.

———. *The Friendly Liquidation of the Past: The Politics of Diversity in Latin America.* Pittsburgh, PA: University of Pittsburgh Press, 2000.

Van Delden, Maarten. "The Survival of the Prettiest: Transmutations of Darwin in José Enrique Rodó's *Ariel*." In *Constellation Caliban: Figurations of a Character*, edited by Nadia Lee and Theo D'haen, 145–161. Amsterdam: Editions Rodopi, 1997.

Vargas Llosa, Mario. "Social Commitment and the Latin American Writer." *World Literature Today* 52, no. 1 (1978): 6–14.

Vaughan, Alden T. "Caliban in the 'Third World': Shakespeare's Savage as Sociopolitical Symbol." *Massachusetts Review* 29, no. 2 (1988): 289–313.

Verdesio, Gustavo. "An Amnesiac Nation: The Erasure of Indigenous Pasts by Uruguayan Expert Knowledges." In *Beyond Imagined Communities: Reading and Writing the Nation in Nineteenth-Century Latin America*, edited by Sara Castro-Klarén and John Charles Chasteen, 196–224. Washington, DC: Woodrow Wilson Center, 2003.

Viotti da Costa, Emilia. "New Publics, New Politics, New Histories: From Economic Reductionism to Cultural Reductionism—In Search of Dialectics." In *Reclaiming the Political in Latin American History: Essays from the North*, edited by Gilbert M. Joseph, 17–31. Durham, NC: Duke University Press, 2001.

Viscardo y Guzmán, Juan Pablo. "An Open Letter to América." In *Latin American Independence: An Anthology of Sources*, edited by Sarah C. Chambers and John Charles Chasteen, 60–66. Indianapolis: Hackett, 2010.

Volek, Emil. "*Nuestra América* / Our America at the Crossroads: Splendors of Prophecy, Misery of History, and Other Mishaps of the Patriotic Utopia (Notes on the Bicentennial Recourse of the Method and on Martí's Blueprint for Macondo)." *Hispanic Issues On Line* 8 (2011): 127–151.

Waisman, Sergio. *Borges and Translation: The Irreverence of the Periphery*. Lewisburg, PA: Bucknell University Press, 2005.

Wallerstein, Immanuel. *Historical Capitalism with Capitalist Civilization*. London: Verso, 1995.

Williams, Raymond L. *The Postmodern Novel in Latin America: Politics, Culture, and the Crisis of Truth*. New York: Palgrave Macmillan, 1995.

Zavala, Iris M. *Colonialism and Culture: Hispanic Modernisms and the Social Imaginary*. Bloomington: Indiana University Press, 1992.

Zavala, Lorenzo de. *Viage a los Estados-Unidos del Norte de América*. Paris: Imprenta de Decourchant, 1834.

Zea, Leopoldo. *Dialéctica de la conciencia americana*. Mexico City: Alianza, 1976.

———. *El pensamiento latinoamericano*. Barcelona: Editorial Ariel, 1976.

———. "El positivismo." In *Pensamiento positivista latinoamericano*, vol. 1, edited by Leopoldo Zea, ix–lii. Caracas: Biblioteca Ayacucho, 1980.

Zea, Leopoldo, and Adalberto Santana, eds. *El 1898 y su impacto en Latinoamérica*. Mexico City: Tierra Firme, 2001.

Zum Felde, Alberto. "La promoción intelectual arielista." In *Indice crítico de la literatura hispanoamericana: Los ensayistas*, 310–330. Mexico City: Editorial Guarania, 1954.

Index